CULTURES OF THE WORLD
Niger

Cavendish
Square
New York

Published in 2020 by Cavendish Square Publishing, LLC
243 5th Avenue, Suite 136, New York, NY 10016
Copyright © 2020 by Cavendish Square Publishing, LLC

Third Edition

Library of Congress Cataloging-in-Publication Data

Names: Seffal, Rabah, author. | Spilling, Jo-Ann, author. | Nevins, Debbie, author.
Title: Niger / Rabah Seffal, Jo-Ann Spilling, and Debbie Nevins.
Description: Third edition. | New York, NY : Cavendish Square Publishing, LLC, 2019. | Series: Cultures of the world | Audience: 6 and up. | Includes bibliographical references and index.
Identifiers: LCCN 2019013494 (print) | LCCN 2019014664 (ebook) | ISBN 9781502647535 (ebook) | ISBN 9781502647528 (library bound)
Subjects: LCSH: Niger--Juvenile literature.
Classification: LCC DT547.22 (ebook) | LCC DT547.22 .S44 2019 (print) | DDC 966.26--dc23
LC record available at https://lccn.loc.gov/2019013494

Writers, Rabah Seffal and Jo-Ann Spilling; Debbie Nevins, third edition
Editorial Director, third edition: David McNamara
Editor, third edition: Debbie Nevins
Art Director, third edition: Alan Sliwinski
Designer, third edition: Jessica Nevins
Production Manager, third edition: Karol Szymczuk
Cover Picture Researcher: Alan Sliwinski
Picture Researcher, third edition: Jessica Nevins

Printed in the United States of America

CONTENTS

NIGER TODAY

THE REPUBLIC OF NIGER IS A HUGE COUNTRY ON A HUGE continent. Yet it occupies a miniscule place in the world's perception. Outside of Africa itself, many people don't know where it is or even what it is. For one thing, Niger is not Nigeria. Google almost anything relating to Niger and the search engine will assume you meant Nigeria. The two countries are neighbors, and their similar names are both derived from the Niger River. But they are not the same country. For another thing, the pronunciation for Niger is not "NYE-djur." The correct way to say it is "nee-ZHAIR."

Niger is a landlocked country in western Africa. It shares borders with several neighbors—Nigeria and Benin to the south, Burkina Faso and Mali to the west, Algeria and Libya to the north, and Chad to the east. For a place that garners little international attention, Niger is nevertheless a country of superlatives. Not only is it one of the largest countries in Africa, it's also one of the hottest places on Earth. More than 80 percent of the country lies within the Sahara Desert. Temperatures can sometimes reach 113 degrees Fahrenheit (45 degrees Celsius).

Many villages in rural regions of Niger look much like this.

Niger also has the sad distinction of being one of the poorest countries in the world. Its economy is mainly based on agriculture, although it has gained from the export of uranium and, more recently, oil. In spite of its natural resources, Niger remains underdeveloped due to its landlocked position, recurring drought, poor infrastructure, and low levels of education among its people. Like many other African nations, the country can trace much of its low economic status and lack of development to a history of oppression and exploitation under European colonialism. In 1960, Niger gained independence from French colonial rule. The French influence is still evident in its official language.

Niger has a rapidly growing population of some twenty million people. Its society is diverse and consists of six major ethnic groups—the Hausa, the Songhai and Zarma (Djerma), the Fulani (Peuhl), the Tuareg, and the Kanuri. The great majority of Nigeriens are Muslims. Most live in rural communities.

Urban dwellers live in the southern cities—the capital, Niamey; and Maradi, Agadez, and Zinder. The north is largely unpopulated desert.

Niger's surging population numbers reflect its high fertility rate. In fact, it has the world's highest fertility rate, with an average of seven children per woman (in 2016). This, in turn, is related to its high rate of child marriage—again the highest in the world, at 76 percent. The (usually forced) marriage of girls below age eighteen—often to much older men—is a common cultural norm. This tradition has the effect of ending girls' education, promoting adolescent motherhood, and producing a great disparity in power between men and women.

In 2016, Save the Children released a report declaring Niger to be the worst place in the world for girls. (Save the Children is an international nongovernmental organization that promotes children's rights and helps

Merchants sell their wares at a market in Niamey.

Young girls in Niamey wear traditional Islamic clothing.

support children in developing countries.) In coming to this conclusion, researchers considered several indicators, including child marriage, adolescent motherhood, education, access to health care, and female representation in government. Of the 144 countries analyzed on the Girls' Opportunity Index, the bottom twenty were all in sub-Saharan Africa. Niger was dead last.

That assessment is only one of many indices that try to evaluate the state of the world's nations. Various organizations conduct their own annual surveys and research to determine the dynamics of global human wealth, health, happiness, and well-being. In 2018, for example, the United Nations Development Programme's Human Development Index ranked Niger 189th out of 189 countries. (For comparison, Norway ranked 1st and the United States ranked 13th.)

As Niger struggles with poverty and its related problems, it also struggles with political instability. Although it has managed to hold elections and conduct peaceful regime change according to its constitution, Niger has also, over the years, suffered dictatorships and multiple coups d'etat (sudden, forceful, and illegal takeovers of the government, typically by the military).

Complicating these woes is Niger's position in the midst of even more politically troubled countries. From Mali to Nigeria to Libya, Niger is surrounded by nations with active, armed separatist insurgencies and civil wars. Jihadi (militant Islamist) terrorist groups occasionally spill across the borders into Niger to carry out bombings and kidnappings. Some of these are aimed against Western interests, particularly French mining operations. Desperate young Nigeriens, lacking food, jobs, and hope, are easily drawn to the revolutionary rhetoric of these jihadi missionaries. Moreover, droves of refugees fleeing violence in neighboring countries cross into Niger, which could not be less equipped to deal with additional needy populations.

As if these problems aren't enough, global climate change is making itself known in Niger in the form of more frequent extremes of weather—flooding and drought. Is there any good news for the Nigerien people? Many international aid organizations are trying to help. For example, the World Bank's International Development Association granted Niger $1 billion to boost its development and to help alleviate poverty. A $437 million Millennium Challenge program focuses on building large-scale irrigation projects, promoting climate-resilient agriculture, and increasing productivity and sales.

Meanwhile, the Nigerien government plans to exploit its oil, gold, coal, and other mineral resources to sustain future growth. If it can avoid corruption and hold off the threats of terrorism, maybe it will succeed. If Niger can throw off the worst of its old, entrenched customs while keeping the best of its cultural heritage, it may yet rise.

GEOGRAPHY

A giraffe family peeks out from beneath some trees in the Koure Giraffe Reserve in Niger.

THE REPUBLIC OF NIGER IS THE sixth-largest country on the continent of Africa, and the second-largest country in West Africa, after Algeria. Its total land area of 488,946 square miles (1.267 million square kilometers) makes it twice the size of Texas and almost twice as large as France. Of the sixteen countries that make up Western Africa, only three are landlocked, and Niger is one of them (Mali and Burkina Faso are the other two).

Niger's seven neighbors include Algeria to the northwest, Libya to the northeast, Chad to the east, Nigeria to the south, Benin and Burkina Faso to the southwest, and Mali to the west.

TOPOGRAPHY

Niger is located north of Africa's belt of tropical forest. Most of the country is desert. Although it is primarily a flat plain, the country has several depressions, plateaus, sandy lowlands, fossilized river valleys, and volcanic mountains.

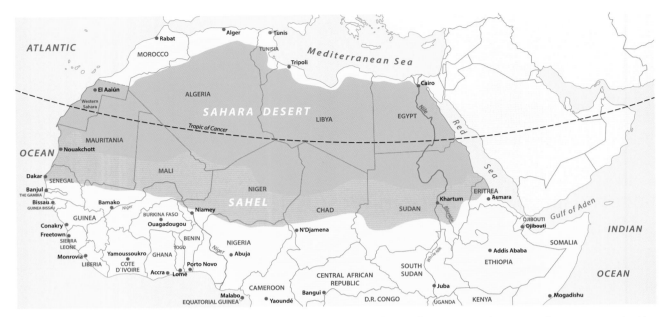

This map shows Niger's position in Africa as well as the Sahara Desert and Sahel zones.

Niger is naturally divided into three distinct regions—a desert zone in the north; an intermediate zone called the Sahelian belt, where nomadic people raise cattle; and a fertile zone in the south. Most of the population lives in this southern region. The country's capital, Niamey, is located in the southwest, on the banks of the Niger River.

THE SOUTH

The Niger River flows across southwestern Niger for some 350 miles (563 kilometers). The fertile region around the river consists of a broad plain with an area of 46,320 square miles (119,969 sq km), or about 10 percent of the total land area of Niger. The altitude in this area varies between 985 and 1,149 feet (between 300 and 350 meters) above sea level. Because it's the country's most intensively cultivated area, some 94 percent of Niger's population lives in the south.

To the southeast, Niger's territory includes 988 square miles (2,559 sq km) of the Lake Chad basin, of what was once Africa's fourth-largest lake. The lake has shrunk by 90 percent since the 1960s, due to climate change, an increase in population, and unplanned irrigation. Whereas the lake once covered parts of southeast Niger, it no longer does. What little remains of the lake lies in Cameroon and Chad.

THE SAHEL

Separating the desert north from the fertile south is the Sahel, an arid region with very little rainfall. The Sahel belt is a geographic zone that spans the entire African continent from the Atlantic Ocean to the Red Sea, covering a large portion of Niger. *Sahel* means "shore" in Arabic—meaning, figuratively, that the area is the shore of the "sea of sand" that is the Sahara.

A dried-up riverbed in the Tahoua region of southern Niger lies in the Sahel belt.

In Niger, this region is usually divided into the north Sahel belt—which includes the city of Agadez, the largest city in central Niger—and the south Sahel belt. In the Agadez region, which is mostly desert, not much will grow except in small oasis towns. The south Sahel belt, meanwhile, has a rainfall pattern that allows crops to be grown for four months of the year. The area also supports grazing for the cattle of nomadic herders. Although the Sahel belts can be relatively self-sufficient in good rainfall years, its inhabitants suffer greatly during severe droughts.

THE NORTH

To the north of the Sahel and the city of Agadez lie the spectacular Aïr (pronounced "eye-ear") Mountains, a southern extension of the Algerian Ahaggar Mountains. Rock paintings made by Stone Age people can be found in this region. With an area of approximately 30,880 square miles (79,979 sq km) and an average elevation of up to 2,625 feet (800 m), the Aïr Mountains are intersected by several ravines where date palms, dum-dum palms, and desert bushes flourish. In the Aïr, Mount Gréboun is Niger's highest peak. It towers at 6,380 feet (1,945 m).

The Sahel region across Africa has long been subject to periodic drought. Between 1911 and 1915, severe drought killed more than 350,000 people in central Niger alone. Another very severe drought occurred in 1968–1973, killing thousands of people, and drought crises have recurred on and off almost every decade since then. In the twenty-first century, droughts hit Niger in 2004–2005, 2010, and most recently (at this writing), in 2017. Indeed, because of climate change, drought is occurring more frequently.

Drought and famine go hand-in-hand in very poor places like Niger because the people have few resources to fall back on. A slight shift in the annual rainy season can mean no precipitation when growing crops need it most. Extreme heat often accompanies prolonged periods of dry weather, exacerbating the problem. Not only do crops die before they can mature, but grasslands shrivel up as well. Livestock and other grazing animals starve to death or die of thirst.

Men unload food aid bags in the village of Doukoukoune, near Maradi, during the famine of 2005.

The worst famines usually occur as a result of several problem situations taking place simultaneously in a kind of "perfect storm." In addition to drought conditions, there may be other forms of natural disasters, such as locust infestations, which wiped out up to 100 percent of crops in parts of Niger in 2005. Severe food shortages can be set off unintentionally by economic market forces, or quite intentionally by political maneuvering. War is a common cause of food insecurity.

Paradoxically, good harvests don't necessarily improve malnutrition conditions in places like Niger. People weakened by malnutrition are extremely vulnerable to diseases, which can become epidemics in the wake of famines. And it can take years to replenish seed stocks and herds of cattle. Extreme poverty is the worst culprit; it is the underlying problem upon which all these other factors take their toll.

East of the Aïr Mountains is the Ténéré, which means "desert" in Tamasheq, the language of the Tuareg people. It's something of a desert within the larger Sahara Desert. The total area of the Ténéré is 154,400 square miles (399,896 sq km). It is a magnificent landscape of sand dunes that seem to stretch to the horizon. This desert is extremely sparsely populated—essentially, not populated at all. Tuareg caravans still traverse it in travel to the oases that punctuate the Ténéré dunes, trading for salt.

To the west of the Aïr, the Talak Desert consists of shifting sand dunes interrupted by ancient river valleys, similar to those found in the Aïr Mountains. About six thousand years ago, water used to flow in these valleys, allowing the desert north of Niger to support a larger population. Now the grasslands of this region attract nomadic cattle herders, but only during the short rainy seasons.

Northeast of the Ténéré lie the high plateaus of Djado and Tchigaï, and the Mangueni Mountains, an extension of the Tibesti Mountains of Chad to the east and the Ahaggar Mountains of Algeria to the north. These highlands form a bridge linking the two mountain systems.

CLIMATE AND RAINFALL

Niger is one of the hottest countries in the world. It has three climatic regions—the desert north, the Sahel, and the south. The desert north, including the Ténéré, receives little rainfall, thus offering neither agricultural nor cattle herding possibilities except in oasis towns and the old river valleys of the Talak Desert, a sandy dune region in western Niger.

South of the desert, the north Sahel has a maximum of 14 inches (36 centimeters) of annual rainfall. In Agadez, annual rainfall does not exceed 7 inches (18 cm). The south Sahel receives 12 to 32 inches (30—81 cm) of rainfall per year. In the south, a rainy season from June to October is preceded by tornadoes. In the extreme south, around Gaya, rainfall averages 32 inches (81 cm) per year.

Temperatures tend to rise again in September and October, during a dry season. From November the temperature starts to drop, as a desert wind, called the harmattan, lowers average temperatures to 70°F (39°C). Reddish sandstorms sweep across the country during this period. From March to June,

Since 1975, the United Nations Educational, Scientific and Cultural Organization (UNESCO) has maintained a list of international landmarks or regions considered to be of "outstanding value" to the people of the world. Such sites embody the common natural and cultural heritage of humanity, and therefore deserve particular protection. The organization works with the host country to establish plans for managing and conserving their sites. UNESCO also reports on sites which are in imminent or potential danger of destruction and can offer emergency funds to try to save the property.

The organization is continually assessing new sites for inclusion on the World Heritage list. In order to be selected, a site must be of "outstanding universal value" and meet at least one of ten criteria. These required elements include cultural value—that is, artistic, religious, or historical significance—and natural value, including exceptional beauty, unusual natural phenomena, and scientific importance.

As of March 2019, there were 1,092 sites listed, including 845 cultural, 209 natural, and 38 mixed properties in 167 nations. Of those, 54 are listed as "in danger." In Niger, three sites are on the main list, including one that is in danger. Niger's World Heritage sites are the W-Arly-Pendjari Complex, which includes the W National Park; the Historic Centre of Agadez, which was added in 2013; and the Aïr and Ténéré Natural Reserves. That site, which is one of the largest protected areas in Africa, is marked as "in danger" because of "political instability and dissention among the populations."

This aerial view shows the city of **Agadez**. The historic section is listed as a **UNESCO** World Heritage site as a "Gateway to the Sahara."

the dry, hot season sets in, with temperatures reaching a scorching 122°F (68°C) in the northeast.

FLORA AND FAUNA

Because of Niger's climate, flora and fauna vary dramatically from the dry north to the wetter and more fertile south. Similar to its Sahelian neighbors, Niger is suffering from ecological degradation. Irregular rainfall and periodic droughts threaten animal populations and plant life of Niger.

The desert north, which covers 60 percent of Niger's land surface, has little vegetation. However, in Bilma, an oasis town in northeast Niger, abundant springs allow some tree species, such as eucalyptus, to flourish. On the northern

The Aïr and Ténéré Natural Reserve is a World Heritage site. UNESCO calls it "the last bastion of Sahara-Sahelian wildlife in Niger."

The fennec is found throughout the African desert region. Its name comes from a Berber word for fox.

rim of the Aïr Mountains, several types of Mediterranean plants, such as olive trees and cypresses, have survived. In the Sahel, scattered pastures of grasses have a short life and provide good grazing material for both nomadic and settled herds. To the south, denser vegetation is found, including baobab trees, silk cotton, mahogany, and shea trees.

In the north the lack of water and vegetation, coupled with extremely high temperatures, limits the types of wildlife. The largest animal found is the one-humped camel. Its broad, leathery footpads are well adapted to the desert. Besides the domesticated camel, wild animals such as antelopes and gazelles are found in the Ténéré and Aïr regions. These animals are the favorite prey of leopards, striped hyenas, and jackals.

The smaller desert animals in Niger include desert foxes, or fennecs, which prey on jerboas or desert mice. The sensitive fennec has large, pointed ears and can hear a desert beetle kick over grains of sand several yards away. Moufflons, a type of small wild sheep, can be found in the inaccessible terrain of the Aïr Mountains and Djado Plateau.

South of the Sahara, ostriches, the world's tallest birds, live in hot, sandy areas. The males are polygamous and travel in multifamily groups. Eggs are laid in sandy depressions and incubated by females during the day and by males at night. Desert animals eat a large number of insects, including the migratory locusts, as well as scorpions and vipers. Although droughts and poaching have taken their toll on Niger's wildlife, some large mammals, such as elephants, giraffes, and hippopotami, and reptiles and amphibians still exist. The nature reserve and wildlife refuge of the W National Park is home to monkeys, baboons, hyenas, jackals, lions, elephants, buffalos, antelopes, and gazelles. Birds, including the brown crow, are also abundant there.

As for domesticated animals, the nomadic peoples herd cattle, sheep, goats, donkeys, and camels. Camels are still used as a means of transportation by

This aerial view shows the flat expanse of Niger's capital city, Niamey, on the Niger River.

caravans, especially by the salt traders, though trucks and jeeps have taken over much of the work.

MAJOR CITIES

NIAMEY   The capital city sits astride the Niger River in southwestern Niger. It wasn't always the capital. In 1926, during the time of French domination, a French general saw the strategic potential of having Niamey as the capital. Access to the river and the moderate climate in this city made the French transfer their administrative capital from Zinder to Niamey. Until then, Niamey was not an economically or politically important city.

Niamey began as a grouping of several villages that grew and joined to become one city. In 1905 the population was only about 1,800. It grew to

Many houses in Zinder, like this one, are decorated with carved and painted designs.

7,000 in 1945. Today, with a population of more than 978,000, Niamey is a sprawling modern center with shantytowns on the outskirts. Beautiful villas can be found in the residential areas next to the ministerial offices. Traditional-style African houses also neatly line the streets.

ZINDER With a population of about 236,000 people, Zinder is a typical Hausa town in south-central Niger, with a narrow maze of alleys. Connected to Niamey by a monotonous 450-mile (724 km) "unity road," it is generally regarded as the second most important city in Niger. Several roads connect Zinder with the city of Kano in Nigeria. A few small industries are located in Zinder. They concentrate on the processing of farm products, such as groundnuts (peanuts) and millet, and the manufacturing of small industrial products.

The neighborhood of Zengou, in Zinder, is a former caravan encampment. Until the 1890s, Zinder was Niger's only major urban settlement, with a population of about 10,000. Built around a citadel, it was a major point of exchange and storage for the trans-Saharan trade route. Precolonial Zinder was called Damagaram, the capital of the Sultanate of Damagaram, a Hausa state and a strong economic power.

In the late nineteenth century, Zinder put up a heavy resistance to the French invasion, ultimately falling in 1899. It remained the administrative capital of the French military territory of Niger until 1926. An old French Foreign Legion fort still stands in the city today.

AGADEZ Located in the Aïr Mountains, about 400 miles (644 km) northeast of Niamey, Agadez was the ancient Tuareg capital. The city still preserves its trading caravans and the myths surrounding that life. It is a town built at the edge of the desert that serves as the link between the free but treacherous desert life and the limited but safe urban life.

The Hausa of the ancient kingdom of Gobir (in what is now Nigeria) fled Tuareg raiders in the sixth century CE and settled in Agadez. The trans-Saharan gold trade route to North Africa passed through Agadez and brought prosperity and strength to local rulers. Beginning in 1325, the Empire of Mali occupied Agadez for fifty years. In 1515, the city fell to the powerful Songhai Empire. Sultans El-Mobarak and Agaba ruled Agadez from 1654 to 1721. In 1906, the French occupied the city.

The desert city of Agadez is constructed of flat-topped earthen brick buildings, a style specific to the Aïr region of Niger.

Today, Agadez is a meeting point for all Tuareg groups and a living center for the preservation of their ancient history. With a population of some 124,325, Agadez is sometimes referred to as the sister city of Timbuktu in Mali. The color of its distinctive sand-brick architecture matches that of the desert dunes. Its people are mainly Tuareg, but the population also includes Fulani nomads and Hausa merchants.

In 2013, its historic center, which dates to the fifteenth and sixteenth centuries, was added to the list of UNESCO World Heritage sites. The site's Grand Mosque is the tallest building ever constructed in mudbrick.

INTERNET LINKS

https://www.britannica.com/place/Niger
This encyclopedia has information on landforms, climate, soils, cities, and plant and animal life in Niger.

**https://www.nationsonline.org/oneworld/map/niger-political
-map.htm**
This site provides excellent political and satellite maps of Niger and its capital.

https://whc.unesco.org/en/statesparties/ne
The World Heritage page for Niger includes links to its three UNESCO sites, as well as nineteen other Nigerien sites on the tentative list.

HISTORY

The ruins of the ancient city of Djado stand
among the date palms in northeastern Niger.
Long abandoned, the ruins date to about eight
hundred to one thousand years ago.

2

NIGER'S HISTORY GOES BACK TO THE earliest days of humankind. Deep in the interior of an enormous continent, the lives of ancient peoples barely changed for thousands of years. But over the long passage of millennia, the desert sands shifted, slowly swallowing up what were once vast expanses of fertile grasslands. Lakes and rivers dried up. Humans and animals fled the desert or learned how to live in it. Empires and kingdoms came and went. Villages and trade routes grew old with use, and life went on.

EARLY INHABITANTS

Stone tools, evidence of a Paleolithic culture, indicate the presence of humans more than sixty thousand years ago in the Aïr, Ténéré, Djado, and Kuwar regions. The stone tools, including axes, oval disks used for cutting and scraping, and stone knives, were produced by a Neolithic Saharan culture that domesticated bulls and herded cattle—an activity that is still practiced today by the different nomadic groups of Niger. People of the Neolithic Saharan culture probably drew the ancient rock

This cave painting clearly shows a hunter encountering a giraffe.

paintings that have been found north of Agadez. The paintings, which date to 3,500—2,500 BCE, portray plants and animals that no longer live in the region. This is evidence of the climatic change that slowly dried out and heated up that part of Africa, leaving the Sahara Desert in its wake.

EARLY EMPIRES

The Kanem Kingdom was located around the Chad Basin from 700 to 1380 CE and occupied a region northeast of Lake Chad called Kanem. Though it was mostly based in the area of what is now the country of Chad, at its height, the kingdom extended into eastern Niger. The Zaghawa people, pre-Islamic inhabitants of the region, were the first to acquire the skills to cast iron, make crafts, and provide services to the nomadic and sedentary groups around Kanem. They relied on agriculture, fishing, and making crafts for a living, and in a later period, they engaged in international trade, which included slaves, with the Muslim states of North Africa and the Middle East. During this time, Muslim traders brought Islam to Kanem.

Around the same time that the Kanem Kingdom was taking hold in the east—the eight century CE—the first Songhai state appeared in the western part of the Niger region. From the core of the earlier Mali Empire, the Songhai Empire expanded its territory along the Niger River, while the Kanem Empire concentrated its rule around Lake Chad and extended its conquest north to the Fezzan in Libya.

In between the two empires, smaller states, such as the Hausa states, emerged. Around 1000 CE, an increase in economic relations with North Africa by way of the Aïr Mountains led to migrations of Tuareg from Libya and Algeria toward the Aïr and adjacent regions. At this time, both the Songhai and Kanem Empires adopted Islam as their religion. Meanwhile, the Hausa, who previously lived in the north, gradually moved south.

Southern Niger was part of west Sudan when gold was traded between the Muslim and Sudanese traders. Although the Muslim traders were involved in the gold trade, their Sudanese counterparts supplied them with little information about the location of the gold mines. Muslim geographers used to say that gold grew in the sand of Sudan as carrots did. The Sudanese had an equally unusual trading relationship with their gold suppliers from the gold-producing center in the south of Niger. Known as the silent auction, this method of barter illustrated their peculiar trading customs.

The Sudanese traders would place their merchandise, mainly salt bars from the Sahara, in piles on the bank of the river and then retreat. Afterward, the local people would appear with their gold and would place some gold next to each pile of merchandise and then withdraw. The traders would return to the riverbank and take the gold if the amount placed against each pile satisfied them. They would then disappear. The local people would emerge from their hiding places and go to the riverbank to collect the merchandise they had bought.

SIXTEENTH TO NINETEENTH CENTURIES

In the sixteenth century, the region that was to become Niger was greatly influenced by the Songhai and Bornu Empires. The Bornu Empire reached its apex under the rule of Idris Alauma (1564—1576). The acme of Songhai rule occurred during the reign of Askia Mohammed (1493—1528). In 1498, Askia Mohammed went on a pilgrimage to the Muslim holy city of Mecca in Arabia. On completing his pilgrimage to Mecca, he received the two honored titles— al Hajj and the Caliph of the Western Sudan—which increased his support among the Songhai Muslims and helped consolidate his rule.

The Songhai Empire was destroyed by Moroccans, who came to search for gold, and who wanted to control the trade routes. The Battle of Tondibi in 1591 was a heavy loss for the Songhai; it was their first encounter with firearms—gunpowder and muskets. Nine years later, the Moroccans were forced out of Dendi. Despite this, the Songhai Askia dynasty soon collapsed and fragmented into smaller and weaker states. The Songhai Empire never regained its previous grandeur.

In the nineteenth century, the Sultanate of Damagaram, founded in 1731, emerged from the old Kanem-Bornu Empire to become a great military and economic power in the east. Zinder was its capital, and manufacturing and new agricultural products were introduced during this period of time.

TUAREG DOMINATION

As a result of an improved economy spurred by the trade routes through the Sahara, the influence of the Tuareg grew. They established their first sultanate in the Aïr Mountains as early as the beginning of the fifteenth century. Agadez, in the southern part of the Aïr Mountains, became an economic and cultural center, attracting merchants from North Africa. As the center grew in economic importance, the role of the Tuareg became more that of an arbiter than a guardian of the caravan traffic. Confederations of Taureg people were able to extend their control to the sedentary south.

This 1860 print from a Parisian magazine shows the old city of Agadez.

THE SCRAMBLE FOR AFRICA

The nations of Africa are a relatively modern creation. As recently as the nineteenth century, vast regions of the continent's interior remained unmapped and unknown to the outside world. Native peoples lived in various tribal kingdoms with their own rich cultures and traditions. But to Europe and the rest of the Western world, Africa was "the dark continent." In this case, "dark" meant not only unexplored but also savage, wild, and uncivilized.

Africa's seacoast regions were more accessible and therefore better known to Europeans. Beginning in the fourteenth century, Portugal and other nations set up trading posts, forts, and attempted colonies along coastal areas. North Africa, however, had long been dominated by Muslim cultures and was essentially a barrier to Europe. Until the eighteenth and nineteenth centuries, European powers were more interested in the Americas.

European colonies in the Americas eventually won their independence. At the same time, the Industrial Revolution was radically changing Western economies and ways of life. For a variety of reasons, Europe took another look at Africa.

Ongoing piracy along the Barbary Coast and a trade dispute between France and Algiers sparked the French invasion of Algiers in 1830. By 1875, the French conquest was complete. Meanwhile, European leaders sent explorers into the heart of Africa to map it, convinced that the African people needed the "civilizing" influence of European culture.

Europe therefore began to see Africa as ripe for the taking, and a virtual land grab began. By 1884–1885, what has come to be called "the Scramble for Africa" was on. A new age of imperialism began in which major Western powers tried to secure and gain supremacy by building an empire of overseas properties. Colonies were a status symbol as well as a source of native resources, labor, and military recruits.

In 1884, thirteen European countries met in Berlin to draw up the rules of African colonization, and to literally split the continent among themselves. Lines of new nations were drawn arbitrarily, sometimes cutting apart historically tribal regions. By 1902, 90 percent of Africa was under European control, with most of the Sahara region— including Niger—belonging to France. By 1914, the European takeover of Africa was complete, with only Ethiopia managing to remain sovereign.

In the Aïr Mountains, from 1654 to 1687, the Tuaregs were ruled by Muhammad al-Mubarak, who extended his authority to the Damergou region of central Niger. He also established a branch of the Agadez dynasty that became the empire of Sarkin Adar in the late seventeenth century. As Tuareg dominance grew, there were frequent internal conflicts, which divided them into several factions. But as they gained control of more regions, they started to appreciate the advantages of being a large-scale organization.

FRENCH CONQUEST

In the nineteenth century, as a prelude to their conquest, Europeans started to explore Niger. In 1890, an agreement between France and Great Britain at a meeting with King Leopold II of Belgium established the border between what was to become Niger and Nigeria. So it was that Niger would become a French territory and Nigeria would be British.

The partitioning of Africa was an attempt to set out spheres of influence and avoid the threat of war among European countries that were eager to gain control over Africa's resources, such as gold and diamonds. France then started its conquest of the country but was met with strong resistance. In 1898, Sultan Ahmadu Kuren Daga ordered the execution of the French explorer Captain Marius Gabriel Cazemajou.

Subsequently, a French armed expedition brutally subdued the resistance, massacring entire villages of people and burning them the ground. Throughout the years of French domination, the local population continued to fight the French. The Zarama uprising (1905—1906) and the Tuareg resistance (1916—1917) resulted in much bloodshed. British troops were brought in to assist the French, and the Tuareg suffered a major defeat. In 1922, when peace was finally restored, Niger became a French colony.

Underneath a portrait of Queen Victoria, Lord Salisbury (*left*) and Paul Cambon examine a map of Africa as part of the Anglo-French Convention of 1898, also known as the Niger Convention. This agreement between Britain and France concluded the partition of West Africa between the colonial powers.

COLONIE DU NIGER

Niger's borders then were not quite the same as they are today. Rather, they were drawn and redrawn as France reconfigured its African possessions. These included its colonial territories of Mauritania, Senegal, French Sudan (now Mali), French Guinea, Côte d'Ivoire (Ivory Coast), Upper Volta (now Burkina Faso), Dahomey (now Benin), and Niger. At its height, the French Empire in Africa was as large in area as the continental United States.

In 1922, Niger's capital was Zinder, the official language was French, and the currency was the French franc. In 1926, the capital was moved to Niamey, which is conveniently located on the Niger River. The French used cooperative local Nigerien chiefs to collect taxes and administer local justice, but all figures of real authority were native French. A governor-general based in Dakar, Senegal, administered the region.

One characteristic of the French colonization was that its colonies were made to pay for the privilege of being a colony. That is, they were expected to provide economic benefits for France, which they would accomplish by increasing the productivity of their natural resources. In arable regions, the French oversaw the farming of groundnuts (peanuts) and cotton. People who couldn't farm were expected to find jobs that paid wages, as opposed to traditional subsistence livelihoods, even if this meant moving to a different part of the country. That way, they could be taxed.

French colonial rule in West Africa was not particularly kind to its subjects. Human rights were not always high on the list of concerns. Although some effort was made to introduce French culture to the Nigeriens and other African subjects through education, the French did not pour a great deal of resources into trying to improve the lives of its colonized peoples.

ROAD TO INDEPENDENCE

After World War II, Europe's age of empire began drawing to a close. France had been decimated by the war, and would soon be further weakened by subsequent wars with its colonies in Indochina and Algeria.

African leaders of Dahomey (now Benin), Upper Volta (now Burkina Faso), Côte d'Ivoire, and Niger pose at the door of the Elysee Palace in Paris after meeting with President Charles de Gaulle of France in 1960 regarding full independence. Niger's Hamani Diori is at the far right.

As France struggled to hold on to its disgruntled colonies, it created the French Union (1946–1958) under a new constitution. French colonies became "overseas territories," and their citizens became French citizens, united as "one France." The former colonies, including Niger, now had representation in the French Parliament, but in actuality, their power and participation were very limited. The African people, for the most part, did not want assimilation into France; they wanted autonomy.

In Niger, a nationalist movement soon gained momentum. In the early 1950s, two groups formed—a radical group with a strong trade union, led by Djibo Bakary; and a more conservative movement, the Nigerien Progressive Party (PPN), that supported Bakary's cousin and political rival Hamani Diori. Diori won the Territorial Assembly elections in 1957. He formed a government and banned Bakary's Sawaba Party.

On September 28, 1958, the Nigerien population, along with voters in most other former French colonies, approved yet another new French constitution. This one created the French Community in place of the French Union. This new arrangement, which provided for autonomy in place of assimilation, grew out of France's war with Algeria (1954–1962)—a conflict France hoped to avoid with its other African territories. On December 19, 1958, Niger's Territorial Assembly voted for Niger to become an autonomous state within the French Community, to be called the Republic of Niger. However, by then the spirit of independence had caught hold and would not be stopped. On August 3, 1960, Niger declared its independence.

AFTER INDEPENDENCE

When Niger gained its independence, Hamani Diori was elected Niger's first president by the country's National Assembly in November 1960. The first Nigerien constitution was approved on November 8, 1960. As the sole party, the PPN became firmly established throughout the country, including the rural areas.

Diori was well respected internationally as a spokesman for African affairs. At home, however, he was criticized for his government's close economic ties with France, which students and unionists called "French neocolonialism." The National Assembly did little more than rubber-stamp Diori's proposals, and his administration was rife with corruption. Diori appointed mostly family members and close friends to his cabinet. He served as his own foreign minister and defense minister. Opposition was suppressed, and being the only candidate in the one-party state, Diori was reelected twice.

When the Sahelian drought of 1968–1973 hit, it led to severe food shortages and dealt a harsh blow to the economy, but Diori's government seemed incapable of doing anything to alleviate the hardship. In fact, his ministers were said to be misappropriating international donations of food aid. Nigeriens grew increasingly dissatisfied with their government.

On April 15, 1974, Lieutenant Colonel Seyni Kountché staged a military coup. He suspended the constitution, dissolved the PPN, and arrested its leaders. However, he freed political prisoners who had been jailed during Diori's reign. Kountché himself replaced Diori. He formed a provisional government, which was led by the Supreme Military Council, and promised fair distribution of food aid. He maintained cordial relations with France despite the fact that he expelled French troops. The late 1980s saw a significant increase in revenue from uranium—which had been discovered in Niger in the 1960s—which allowed Niger to recover financially from the drought.

Following Kountché's death in 1987, Colonel Ali Seybou was appointed president. In 1993, Mahamane Ousmane became president in the country's first multiparty presidential elections. He, in turn, was ousted in a 1996 military coup by Colonel Ibrahim Baré Maïnassara, putting an end to the short-lived democracy.

Maïnassara was elected president in July in an election reportedly marred by fraud. His time in power would not last long. Maïnassara was assassinated by his own presidential guard on April 9, 1999, at the Niamey airport while he was trying to board a flight to flee the country. Prime Minister Ibrahim Assane Mayaki dismissed Maïnassara's death as a "tragic accident." A

For more than a century, Berber separatists have fought on and off to establish an independent Berber state. The Berber people are descendants of the pre-Arab inhabitants of North Africa. Today, many live in parts of Algeria and Morocco, and to a lesser extent, in Libya.

The Tuareg are a large, traditionally nomadic Berber tribe who live in the Sahara and Sahel regions. The 1884 European carving-up of Africa drew borders through the caravan routes they had worked for centuries, dividing them up between Mauritania, Algeria, Libya, Mali, Niger, and Chad. They have staged various insurgencies dating back to 1916.

Tuareg rebels fight during a 1994 revolt in northern Niger.

In the 1990s, Tuaregs rebelled in Niger for more autonomy from the Nigerien government, which is based many hundreds of miles away and dominated by ethnic black Africans. The Tuaregs complained of being impoverished and marginalized. They were not benefiting from the wealth of uranium being extracted from their lands, much of which went to foreign owners. Both parties consequently signed several peace treaties granting Tuareg communities a greater degree of autonomy and greater representation in Niger's government. But the truces were short-lived. In 2007–2009, another rebellion broke out in northern Niger, claiming, in part, that the previous accords were not being honored.

The latest uprising, the ongoing Tuareg Rebellion of 2012, is based in Mali, but it tends to spill over into Niger. Organized under the umbrella group National Movement for the Liberation of Azawad (MNLA), a movement founded in 2011, the mostly Tuareg fighters have raised rebellion to a dangerous new level. Some two thousand to three thousand Tuareg men—mostly from Mali, but some from Niger—became battle-hardened fighting in Libya's ongoing civil war (2011–present). They returned home better trained, armed, and equipped.

National Reconciliation Council was formed, and in October 1999, Mamadou Tandja from the National Movement for the Development of Society (MNSD) Party was elected president.

TWENTY-FIRST CENTURY

Mamadou Tandja was reelected in 2004, but his second term was complicated by a new outbreak of insurgency among the Tuareg in 2007. Tandja declared a state of alert in the Agadez region, giving the security forces extra powers to fight the insurgency. Newspapers were shut down, and journalists were threatened and arrested. In 2009, Tandja suspended the nation's constitution and assumed emergency powers. He sought to extend his presidency beyond 2009, which was the constitutional limit. He continued as president until 2010.

President Mahamadou Issoufou delivers a speech at the presidential palace in Niamey on February 26, 2016.

In February 2010, Tandja was ousted in a military coup d'etat. A senior military officer, Colonel Salou Djibo, took over but promised a return to democratic government. In 2011, longtime opposition leader Mahamadou Issoufou was elected president, ending a year-long military junta. He was reelected in a runoff election in March 2016. However, supporters of his opponent, former prime minister Hama Amadou, boycotted the election in protest after their candidate was imprisoned. The next presidential election is scheduled for 2021.

CONFLICTS NEXT DOOR

Meanwhile, tensions in Niger have run high as conflicts in neighboring Mali, Nigeria, Libya, and Chad threaten the border regions. In all of these countries, separatist insurgencies, civil wars, and international jihadi terrorist groups are active, and Niger is vulnerable on many fronts. The rebel causes attract many disaffected young Nigerien men who are frustrated by the poverty and lack of opportunity in their lives. As a result, various terrorist events and kidnappings of foreign nationals have occurred in Niger in recent years.

Displaced children fill their cans with water from a water fountain in a refugee camp near Diffa in southeastern Niger in 2016.

In addition, people fleeing from violence in those neighboring countries have flocked to Niger, setting up refugee camps in border towns that cannot afford the burden. Desperate migrants hoping to get to Europe are channeled through Agadez in search of smugglers.

FOREIGN MILITARY PRESENCE

In an effort to suppress and defeat terrorist and extremist militant organizations such as al-Qaeda, ISIS (Islamic State), Boko Haram, and the MNLA, several foreign nations have sent troops to Niger. In 2013, suicide bombers associated with a jihadist group attacked a Nigerien army barracks in Agadez and a French-owned uranium mine in Arlit. Twenty-three soldiers were killed in Agadez, along with one staff member at the mine. Fourteen mine workers were injured, and the facilities were seriously damaged. The terrorists released a statement saying they were specifically targeting French interests in Niger.

In 2014, France set up Operation Barkhane throughout Africa's Sahel region. Three thousand French security troops were permanently stationed in five countries referred to as the "G5 Sahel"—Burkina Faso, Chad, Mali, Mauritania, and Niger. The troops have been involved in numerous battles with jihadists. Germany and Italy also sent troops to the Niger region to support counterterrorist operations.

The United States sent one hundred military personnel to Niger in 2013. As of 2018, that number had risen to eight hundred Special Operations troops. The US military also began building a massive drone base outside Agadez. Most Americans were unaware of US involvement in Niger until October 2017, when four US Green Berets were ambushed and killed near the desert town of Tongo Tongo by Islamic State fighters. Four Nigerien soldiers and an interpreter were also killed in the attack.

INTERNET LINKS

https://www.bbc.com/news/world-africa-13944995
This timeline includes Niger's important events beginning in 1890.

https://www.britannica.com/place/Niger
This encyclopedia offers information on Niger's history, starting from the fourteenth century.

https://www.brookings.edu/blog/order-from-chaos/2017/06/13/ in-the-eye-of-the-storm-niger-and-its-unstable-neighbors
This article provides a good look at the insurgencies threatening Niger from neighboring countries.

https://www.migrationpolicy.org/article/tuareg-migration-critical -component-crisis-sahel
This in-depth article delves into the source of Tuareg discontent that has led to rebellion in Niger and Mali.

GOVERNMENT

President Mahamadou Issoufou waves the Nigerien national flag during a 2015 protest in Niamey against deadly raids by the terror group Boko Haram.

THE REPUBLIC OF NIGER BECAME AN independent nation on August 3, 1960. It's a semi-presidential republic—the president is the chief of state; the prime minister is the head of government. The capital is Niamey, Niger's largest city, which is located in the southwestern part of the country and makes up a special capital district. In addition, the country has seven administrative regions—Agadez, Diffa, Dosso, Maradi, Tahoua, Tillabéri, and Zinder.

THE CONSTITUTION

On November 8, 1960, the constitution of the newly independent Niger was officially published, establishing a presidential regime. Following the coup in 1974, this constitution was suspended, and the National Assembly was dissolved. All executive and legislative power was held by the Supreme Military Council until 1989. In 1993 a new constitution was adopted. When the government was overthrown by Colonel Ibrahim Maïnassara in 1996, the constitution was revised by national referendum.

3

The flag of Niger has three equal horizontal bands of orange, white, and green, with a small orange circle centered in the white band. Although it is not stated officially, the orange band is said to stand for the dry northern regions of the Sahara, the white stands for purity, and the green symbolizes hope as well as the fertile southern part of the country. The orange circle represents the sun.

In July 2009, changes were made to Niger's constitution to allow President Mamadou Tandja to remain in office past his term limit. That prompted protests from some parts of Nigerien society and eventually led to a military coup d'etat in 2010. Rebel soldiers attacked and deposed him, establishing a temporary military junta called the Supreme Council for the Restoration of Democracy (CSRD) with the goal of establishing a more democratic government.

As of 2019, "the seventh republic" of Niger operated under the constitution of October 31, 2010. This new constitution, which returned the country to civilian rule, was adopted by referendum with 90.2 percent in favor, with a 52 percent voter turnout. The constitution granted amnesty to the "authors, co-authors and accomplices" of the 2010 coup d'etat.

The Nigerien constitution separates church and state, and guarantees the political, cultural, and religious freedom of its citizens, with the right to form associations. Under the constitution, all languages have equal status as national languages, although French is the official language. Nigeriens have the freedom to travel in and out of the country. Under the new constitution, suspects cannot be arrested without due process of the law.

THE PRESIDENT

The president serves for five years, for a maximum of two terms. Elected by popular vote, the president is the chief of state. He appoints a prime minister and a cabinet of ministers on the recommendation of the prime minister.

In 2011, Mahamadou Issoufou (b. 1952) won the presidential election. He was reelected in 2016. In the February 2016 election, he faced fourteen challengers and won slightly more than 48 percent of the vote. The Niger presidential election system requires an absolute majority win; therefore, a runoff was required. So Issoufou and his nearest challenger, the former prime minister Hama Amadou, who had won about 17 percent, advanced to a second round of elections the following month. However, Amadou's supporters boycotted the runoff election to protest his imprisonment on allegedly trumped-up, politically motivated charges. That helped to clinch a landslide victory for Issoufou, who then won about 92 percent of the vote.

THE LEGISLATIVE BRANCH

The legislature is the unicameral, or one-house, National Assembly. In 2016, the number of seats in this legislative body was increased from 113 to 171. As such, 158 members are directly elected from eight multi-member constituencies in the seven administrative regions and Niamey according to party-list proportional representation. Eight seats are reserved for minorities elected in special single-seat constituencies by a simple majority vote, and five seats are reserved for Nigeriens living abroad—one seat per continent.

The National Assembly is headed by the prime minister, who is appointed by the president and authorized by the assembly. In 2011, Brigi Rafini (b. 1953), a Tuareg, was appointed prime minister, and he was reappointed in 2016. He is to serve until the next presidential election in 2021.

Cars and bikes pass by the National Assembly in Niamey on February 22, 2010, a few days after a military coup that overthrew Niger's president Mamadou Tandja.

THE JUDICIAL BRANCH

According the Niger's constitution, the country's court system operates independently of the executive and legislative branches. However, rulings by the highest courts are often ignored by the high ranking politicians, including those in the executive branch.

Despite allegations of corruption among the judges, Niger's court system reportedly enjoys a relatively high degree

Prior to the country's 2016 presidential election, supporters of Niger's opposition party rally in Niamey. The banner reads, "The people stand for the alternating democracy with a clean record and an impartial constitutional court."

of public trust, compared to those of other African nations. The biggest public complaint, echoed by international observers, is that the justice system is very slow, overburdened, and inefficient. Part of the problem is that there are few lawyers in Niger, which not only slows the processes of justice but drives up the price for legal representation and therefore makes it inaccessible to large portions of the population.

Structurally, there are four high courts—the Constitutional Court, the High Court of Justice, the Supreme Court, and the Court of State Security.

The Constitutional Court consists of seven judges who rule on constitutional and electoral matters. They are nominated as follows: one by the president of the republic, one by the president of the National Assembly, two by peer judges, two by peer lawyers, one by peer law professors, and one from within Nigerien society. All are then appointed by the president. They serve for six-year terms, with terms overlapping so that every two years, one or two new members join the court.

The High Court of Justice also has seven judges, and they deal with cases involving senior government officials. These justices serve five-year terms and are selected from among the legislature and judiciary.

Subordinate courts include the Court of Cassation (an appeals court), the Council of State, the Court of Finances, various specialized tribunals, and the customary regional courts for deciding cases involving the usual breaches of law.

Since 2013, the president of the Constitutional Court has been a woman, Abdoulaye Ly Diori Kadidiatou (b. 1952). She holds a doctorate in public law from the University of Paris and is known for her activism in women's organizations. She was appointed to the court by President Mahamadou Issoufou in 2013 and was elected its president by the other justices that same year.

She is the second female chief justice to hold this position, the first being Salifou Fatimata Bazèye (b. 1951), who held the post from 2007 to 2009. Then, following the 2010 coup d'etat, she headed the transitional Constitutional Court. In 2011, Bazèye was chosen as "African of the Year" by the news publisher Media Trust Limited. The awards committee cited her "track record as an incorruptible judicial officer."

It was Bazèye who delivered the judicial ruling against President Mamadou Tandja in 2009, when he proposed to amend the constitution to allow for his continued reign beyond the two-term limit. Tandja then dismissed Bazèye from her position for taking this uncompromising stance of upholding the law, but he would lose in the end. Bazèye is credited with playing a key role in steering Niger to a successful election and democratic transition following Tandja's ouster.

CITIZENSHIP

Being born in Niger is not enough to qualify a person for citizenship. At least one parent must be a Nigerien citizen. Until 2014, that parent had to be the father, but an amendment to the constitution removed that instance of gender inequality and allowed women to pass on their nationality as well. However, in rural areas, in particular, birth registration is spotty, and therefore citizenship can be difficult to prove.

THE MILITARY

Niger's armed forces (FAN) consist of the Niger Army and the Niger Air Forces. As a landlocked country, Niger does not have a navy. Paramilitary branches include the national police (National Gendarmerie) and the National Guard. The National Gendarmerie's mission is to provide police protection outside

Niger continues to experience terrorist acts from organizations based outside the country. Although Niger has no homegrown terror group within its territory, several militant groups operate along its borders, threatening its security. Native Nigeriens do join them. Disaffected young men growing up in poverty and oppression, without hope of a better future, are often attracted by the fiery jihadist rhetoric. The main terror groups operating as threats to Niger are these:

***Al-Mulathamun Battalion**—It seeks to "unite all Muslims from the Nile to the Atlantic in jihad against Westerners."*
> *Base—Mali*
> *Goals—To replace several African governments, including Niger's government, with an Islamic state.*
> *Areas of operation—Algeria, Burkina Faso, Libya, Mali, and Niger. It conducts attacks against Nigerien military and security personnel, and targets Westerners for kidnappings for ransom.*

***Jama'at Nasr al-Islam wal-Muslimin (JNIM)**—Affiliated with al-Qaeda, it seeks to incite the West African Muslim community to "remove oppression" and expel non-Muslim "occupiers" [France and its allies].*
> *Base—Mali*
> *Goal—To establish an Islamic state, based on sharia law, centered in Mali.*
> *Areas of operation—Primarily based in northern and central Mali. The group targets Western and local interests in West Africa and the Sahel, and has claimed responsibility for attacks in Mali, Niger, and Burkina Faso.*

***Boko Haram**—Jihadist group violently opposed to any political or social activity associated with Western society, including voting, attending secular schools, and wearing Western dress.*
> *Base—Northeastern Nigeria*
> *Goal—To establish an Islamic caliphate across Africa.*
> *Areas of operation—Nigeria, Chad, Niger, and Cameroon. It conducts kidnappings, bombings, and assaults, and is responsible for displacing thousands of people and contributing to food insecurity.*

of urban areas. The army and air force operate under the Ministry of Defense, while the national police and national guard are under the Ministry of the Interior.

There are about twelve thousand active duty personnel and five thousand reservists in total. Eighteen is the legal minimum age for compulsory or voluntary military service; enlistees must be Nigerien citizens and unmarried. They serve for two years. Women are allowed to serve only in duties related to health care.

Niger's military budget totals only about 1.6 percent of government expenditures. Most of Niger's military equipment comes from France, with which it has bilateral defense agreements.

In Agadez, soldiers parade during a ceremony marking the anniversary of the Nigerien republic on December 18, 2016.

INTERNET LINKS

https://www.constituteproject.org/constitution/ Niger_2010?lang=en
The 2010 version of Niger's constitution is presented on this site.

https://www.nationsonline.org/oneworld/niger.htm
This site provides up-to-date information about Niger's government.

ECONOMY

The West African franc is the currency
of eight nations, including Niger.

4

N IGER HAS ONE OF THE WORLD'S largest uranium deposits—about 7 percent of Earth's total amount—and is the fourth-largest producer of the ore. The country also has gold and silver mines, and produces crude oil. Yet Niger is one of the world's poorest countries. What accounts for this seeming paradox? The answer explains a great deal about the nation's economic situation.

A $437 million Millennium Challenge Corporation compact, entered into force in January 2018, will strengthen Niger's agricultural sector by improving water availability, roads, and market access.

AGRICULTURE

More than 80 percent of the Nigerien population works in agriculture and in raising livestock. Crops are grown mainly in the south where rainfall is more abundant and the soils are richer. Most farms are small, family-owned plots of about 12 acres (5 hectares) or less, worked by hand or with animals. Most farming is not mechanized or irrigated, and is therefore wholly dependent on rainfall. Most farmers grow only enough to feed their families.

The dry north and Sahel areas, which receive only seasonal rainfall, are used for nomadic livestock-raising. Successive droughts in 1971, 1984, and more recently in 2004—2005, 2010, and 2012 considerably reduced the size of the cattle herds.

A Nigerien man inspects lettuce crops on the fertile banks of the Niger River close to Niamey.

Groundnuts, or peanuts, are planted in the sandy soils of Maradi and Zinder. Cowpeas and onions are grown for commercial export, mainly to Nigeria, as are limited quantities of garlic, pepper, gum arabic, and sesame seeds. To diversify the economy and reduce Niger's dependence on peanuts, cotton was introduced as a crop in 1956. It is cultivated in the Tahoua region but remains a small part of the agricultural output. Niger's main food crops are sorghum and millet, which are grown on about 90 percent of the cultivated land. Millet is usually grown by itself in light soil, but sometimes it is planted among rows of peanuts or beans. Sorghum requires a richer soil than millet. A small portion of the millet and sorghum production is exported.

Niger does not grow enough food to feed its rapidly growing population. It imports grains, including wheat, rice, corn, millet, and sorghum. The harvest varies as much as 10 percent from year to year, depending on the amount of rainfall—production can fall by as much as 40 percent during the drought years and, correspondingly, it can yield more in the good rainfall years. Most of the rice produced is consumed locally. As demand for cassava and beans has increased, cultivation of these crops has grown. Nigeriens also grow tomatoes, wheat, and sugarcane. Most of the sugarcane plantations are located near Tillabéri. Wheat is grown in Agadez, near Lake Chad, and in the Aïr and Kuwar Mountains. Tomatoes grow well in Tahoua, Zinder, and Agadez.

HUSBANDRY AND FISHING

Animal husbandry is Niger's most important activity. Land that is unsuitable for agriculture, but not totally desert, is used for grazing animals. Herds traditionally move north during the rainy season. The animals are the herders'

Gross domestic product (GDP) is a measure of a country's total production. The number reflects the total value of goods and services produced over one year. Economists use it to determine whether a country's economy is growing or contracting. Growth is good, while a falling GDP means trouble. Dividing the GDP by the number of people in the country determines the GDP per capita (per person). This number provides an indication of a country's average standard of living—the higher the better.

In 2017, the GDP per capita in Niger was approximately $1,200. That figure is extremely low, and it ranked Niger 224th out of 229 countries listed by the CIA World Factbook. (For comparison, the United States that year was number 19, with a GDP per capita of $59,500; Niger's neighbor Nigeria was number 166 with $5,900.)

capital and only resource. Used for transportation, the animals also provide milk, meat, and leather. The leather is used for the awnings of tents, clothes, shoes, and ropes. In a good year, communities can perform social and religious activities, such as making donations and making sacrifices.

The main herd animal is the zebu. It's a member of the ox family, characterized by curved horns shaped like a harp and a relatively large, fleshy hump over its shoulders. The zebu has pendulous ears and a distinct resistance to heat and insect attacks. Other herd animals include goats, sheep, and camels.

Fishing activities take place along the banks of the Niger River and near Lake Chad.

A zebu stands on the side of a road.

MINING AND INDUSTRY

In 1960 Niger started a program to develop its mineral resources. As a result, uranium was discovered at Arlit in the Agadez region in 1967. Huge coal reserves were also discovered northeast of Agadez.

To understand the relationship between Niger and uranium, it helps to know what uranium is. A naturally occurring element found in Earth's crust, uranium is an extremely dense, silvery metal found in tiny amounts in certain minerals. When it comes into contact with air, it quickly forms a thin black layer of oxidation on its surface.

Uranium ore can be mined by various methods, depending on its depth in the ground. After mining, the ore is crushed, ground up, and treated with acid. This dissolves the uranium, which is then recovered from solution. The end product of the mining and milling stages is uranium oxide concentrate (U3O8). This is the form in which uranium is sold.

Trucks carry rocks containing uranium in an open mine in the Arlit region.

In ancient times, uranium was used to make orange and yellow colors in glass and ceramic glazes. That was long before people came to understand the element's radioactive properties, which were discovered by a French physicist in 1896.

Understanding radioactivity requires some knowledge of chemistry and physics—particularly the properties of atoms. Essentially, a material is radioactive if it gives off energy in the form of invisible tiny particles or rays. Radiation enables powerful technologies. On the other hand, radiation is hazardous to living things.

Today, the main use of uranium is as a fuel in nuclear power plants. Just a small amount can produce a huge amount of energy. In fact, 2.2 pounds (1 kilogram) of uranium can produce as much energy as 1,500 tons (1,360 metric tons) of coal. Uranium also has military uses—for example, in the creation of nuclear weapons. Depleted uranium (DU), a less radioactive byproduct of nuclear reactions, is used to make bullets and larger projectiles. Uranium's density makes ammunition hard enough to punch through armored targets. It's also used to improve the metal armor used on tanks and other armored vehicles.

Uranium is a toxic metal. It can cause cancer in human beings and serious damage to the environment. There are different degrees of radioactivity, and increased exposures increase the harm it can cause.

After the discovery of uranium in the 1960s, Niger enjoyed large export earnings that significantly benefited its economy. Money was channeled to the development of infrastructure, industry, communications, and training. However, in the early 1980s, the oversupply and falling prices of uranium adversely affected the economy.

Besides mining in the north, Niger's industrial production includes a manufacturing industry in the south, where factories process agricultural products, such as peanuts, millet, sorghum, cotton, and cattle products. Smaller industrial units focus on making cement and mortar bricks for local consumption.

Recently, deposits of gold have also been found in Niger, in the region between the Niger River and the border with Burkina Faso. In 2004, President Tandja announced the official opening of the Samira Hill Gold Mine, the first commercial gold production facility, in the region of Tera. Significant deposits of phosphates, iron, limestone, and gypsum have also been found in Niger. Mining operations have also discovered copper, lignite, zinc, chromium, molybdenum, tungsten, lithium, and titanium.

TRANSPORTATION

Because it has no railroads or ports, Niger relies on roads for transportation. Niger's road grid includes east-to-west and north-to-south roads that provide access to neighboring countries. The main roads include those from Niamey to Zinder, Tahoua, Arlit, and Gaya. Many other roads may only be traveled after gaining special permission from the government of Niger. Many secondary roads are made of dirt and gravel, which can be impassable after heavy rains. The total length of highways is 11,774 miles (18,949 km), of which only 2,430 miles (3,912 km) are paved.

Niger has two international airports: Diori Hamani International Airport, serving Niamey; and Mano Dayak International Airport, serving the city of Agadez. Flights from the United States must connect in Europe. Air France is the only European carrier that flies to Niger. Other than that, it is only possible to

Niger's two main uranium mines, Somaïr and Cominak, are located in the remote desert town of Arlit. The mines are owned by Areva, a majority state-owned French company and one of the largest uranium producers in the world. And France is the main buyer of the uranium that comes out of those mines. In fact, one-third of all electricity in France is produced by uranium from Niger. Meanwhile, a mere 15 percent of Nigeriens have access to electricity, none of it from nuclear power. France, therefore, clearly benefits from Nigerien uranium, but how much does Niger benefit?

Miners work underground in an Arlit uranium mine.

The precise answer is hard to determine, as the contracts between Niger and Areva are not public—this despite Niger's 2010 constitution, which mandates the publication of natural resources contracts. However, it's well known that Niger gets a very small, variable royalty of between 5.5 and 12 percent.

The people in the Arlit area are desperately poor and have to buy a daily allotment of water. The mines, however, use enormous amounts of water in their operations and have depleted an ancient aquifer deep below the sands.

There have been no official, large-scale health studies conducted in Arlit, but a number of environmental organizations, including Greenpeace, claim the uranium mining there has deeply poisoned the environment and the town's 120,000 people.

But the danger in Arlit doesn't stop there. The surrounding area is notorious for its bandits and armed groups, including Islamist militants. A number of militant attacks and kidnappings have occurred in the area, including some directly targeting Areva. In 2010, seven of the company's employees were abducted, including five French nationals. In 2013, an attack on the Somaïr mine left one dead and sixteen injured.

access the country via regional and neighboring capitals. The national airline, Niger Airlines, offers domestic air services between Diffa, Maradi, and Zinder. It has two aircraft in its fleet. Air Niamey was a charter service that has turned into a scheduled carrier. In addition, Niger Air Base 201, a US air base in Agadez for armed drone missions and other aircraft, was expected to be completed in 2019. However, this base is for the use of the US military only.

To transport goods overseas, Niger uses the Cotonou port in Benin and the Lagos port in Nigeria. Between December and March, the Niger River is navigable for 186 miles (300 km) from Niamey to Gaya, which lies on the border with Benin. Canoes are used to ferry people across rivers. In the rural areas, where road networks are less developed, donkeys and camels are used. It is not unusual to see camels crossing the bridges in the capital city of Niamey.

A man walks a camel carrying a large bundle of herbs across a bridge over the Niger River in December 2017 in Niamey.

Drivers pull out of a gas station in Niamey.

ENERGY RESOURCES

OIL   Niger has a huge oil potential. It only began producing oil in 2011, with the opening of the Agadem oil field in the southeast, north of Chad. Oil from that field is transported through a 265-mile (426.5 km) underground pipeline to a refinery in Zinder. Most of that oil goes toward supplying domestic power.

Foreign companies, such as China National Petroleum Corporation, have taken notice of Niger's oil potential, and have signed exploration and production contracts with the Nigerien government. As a result of new exploratory wells, Niger's potential reserves have been found to be significantly higher than previously estimated. In 2018, the UK-based oil and gas company Savannah Petroleum announced the discovery of three oil reserves in the Agadem Rift Basin.

HYDROELECTRIC In 2008, the government began building a dam on the Niger River near the town of Kandadji in the Tillabéri region. The Kandadji Dam will serve several purposes, including generation of hydroelectric power. Construction has taken longer than expected and as of 2018, completion was expected in 2020. The Office of Solar Energy is producing solar batteries, which are used to power the country's telecommunications network.

INTERNET LINKS

https://africanarguments.org/2017/07/18/a-forgotten-community -the-little-town-in-niger-keeping-the-lights-on-in-france-uranium -arlit-areva
This article reveals alarming information about the Areva uranium mine's impact on the town of Arlit.

https://www.geopoliticalmonitor.com/uranium-in-niger-when-a- blessing-becomes-a-curse
This opinion piece explores the unbalanced relationship between Niger and France when it comes to uranium.

https://tradingeconomics.com/niger/indicators
This site provides up-to-date statistics on Niger's economy and related issues.

ENVIRONMENT

An uda, a breed of sheep commonly raised in the Sahel region, grazes in the Niger River meadows close to Niamey.

5

NIGER HAS EXPERIENCED EXTREME drought, food shortages, and increased desertification over the last forty years. Food insecurity and drought have long been recurrent problems for the country, but they have been exacerbated by global climate change, careless use of scant natural resources, and high population growth. In the mid-2000s, Nigeriens suffered terribly from a food crisis bordering on famine. These factors also place severe pressure on the environment. Living in this fragile environment, many people in Niger feel as though they are never far from disaster.

Besides the main concerns of desertification and drought, Niger's other environmental issues today include overgrazing, soil erosion, deforestation, and threats to its wildlife population. The government has demonstrated its commitment by increased investment in the national budget to be spent on useful projects to help the environment. It is evident that the government and other politicians take Niger's environmental concerns very seriously, as the recent elections have been fought over these pressing environmental issues.

Drought is probably the greatest climate-related threat to Niger, resulting in widespread food insecurity. Lower crop production in drought years means higher prices, which the already impoverished Nigeriens cannot afford. Drought also affects livestock herds, weakening and killing the animals the people rely on for meat and milk.

However, the serious problem of nuclear pollution in the uranium mining region of Arlit receives little notice, and even denials by both the Nigerien government and the French-owned mining company. As yet, there hasn't been a sufficient study of the increasing illnesses and deaths in the town, and reports are mostly anecdotal. Nevertheless, the environmental and human toll of the mining appears to be devastating.

DESERTIFICATION

As in many parts of the world, desertification has posed a threat to the Sahel. The desert already occupies over 80 percent of Niger. But in the 1990s, it was reported that 965 square miles (2,500 sq km) of land were being lost each year in Niger through desertification.

Desertification is caused mainly by the reckless use of land—for example, overgrazing and slash-and-burn techniques in agriculture. A century ago, people in the Sahel did farm the land, but their agricultural practices were balanced by hunting activities. They were able to feed their families by hunting for lions, elephants, giraffes, ostriches, addaxes, antelopes, and deer for meat and hides.

In colonial times, farmers in the south of Niger were actively encouraged to cultivate land commercially to produce peanuts for export. The growth of the peanut industry has resulted in the rapid destruction of stable perennial vegetation. This, in turn, has caused widespread desertification.

Today, farmers rely solely on agriculture for their livelihoods. In the Sahel, farmers have used brutal slash-and-burn methods to clear natural forests and bushland for agricultural use. The destruction of the vegetation causes the land to be exposed and soil erosion to occur, leaving the land barren and infertile. Fortunately for the large percentage of Nigeriens who rely on agriculture for survival, there is a natural greenbelt situated north of the town of Tânout that protects the farmers from the Sahara Desert. This area is rich with perennials and even wildlife such as gazelles and desert partridges. The flora and fauna offer protection to the area by fending off wind and water erosion.

In spite of the fact that parts of Niger have already suffered greatly from the negative effects of desertification, researchers were surprised and impressed to discover that, since the mid-2000s, the situation has improved dramatically. In some areas, farmers have even managed to halt the process of desertification almost completely. By implementing basic preventative techniques such as planting trees and preserving natural vegetation, approximately 11.6 million square miles (30 million sq km) of severely degraded land have been successfully rehabilitated, according to the Nigerien government. As a result of massive tree-planting programs, there is an abundance of new trees in certain parts of southern Niger.

Wrapped tree saplings await planting in the fight against desertification.

These antidesertification programs are good news for the environment as well as for the economy, as tens of thousands of people will gain employment to carry out the work of replanting and reforesting. In 2006, the government pledged the equivalent of about $2.8 million each year to tackle the problems of desertification, including restoring damaged lands, sand dunes, and oasis water. Niger's success at restoring its environment against desertification is an encouraging model for what can be achieved by simple means combined with government support. Niger's reforestation programs have the full backing of the government.

It is impressive that, through the efforts made in its antidesertification programs, Niger now has the problem of desertification under control and is carrying out further improvements for the future. Niger's farmers are delighted with the results, as this means they can once again make a living from the land and be independent. This can be clearly seen by the vast increase in the production of one of Niger's most important cash crops, the onion. In 2005, it was reported that, in the last twenty years, onion production had tripled to 297,624 tons (270,000 metric tons), which were exported mainly to Nigeria and Benin. Combating the effects of desertification has enhanced the quality of life for farmers and their families in Niger. A few of the more important benefits can be seen in the decrease in child mortality and the ability of some farmers to send their children to school to receive an education. However, these improvements may be short-lived if the birthrate continues to increase at its current explosive rate. It is estimated that Niger's population will rise to 56 million by 2050, compared with 16 million in 2010 and 20.5 million in 2020. Experts are also quick to offer reminders that Niger still suffers from other environmental issues, which contribute to its food crisis, including climate change, erratic rainfall, and soil degradation.

THE GREENING OF THE SAHEL

Curiously, the fight against desertification in some regions is getting help from an unlikely source—global warming and climate change. Earth Observation (EO) studies generally show a positive trend in rainfall and vegetation greenness over recent decades for the majority of the Sahel—not only in Niger—that has been dubbed "the greening of the Sahel."

Changing weather patterns are evident in the increase of extreme weather events—including more frequent droughts—in recent years. If the Sahel becomes much rainier, it could be good news for agriculture, industry, and domestic use. But very erratic weather—extreme droughts followed by destructive floods—would surely complicate those benefits.

THREATS TO WILDLIFE

As in many other African countries, Niger's wildlife population is under severe threat mainly because of the illegal practice of poaching and the destruction of natural habitats. Animals that are endangered in Niger today include giraffes, elephants, hippopotami, lions, and some others. The country's northern deserts have been popular hunting grounds for wealthy Middle Easterners and others, with large entourages and sophisticated weapons to track and kill the animals.

In 2001, Niger introduced a hunting ban in an effort to save its wildlife population, but enforcement is lax. And, as is often the case in desperately poor countries, a great many impoverished Nigeriens don't see the value of preserving their own wildlife when it could be a source of food or income.

One of the animals facing critical threat is the addax, also called the white antelope. The IUCN (International Union for Conservation of Nature) Red List

The Niger food crisis of 2005 mainly affected the regions of northern Maradi, Tahoua, Tillabéri, and Zinder. Several factors contributed to making this the country's worst food crisis yet—an unexpected and premature termination to the rains in 2004, a fierce attack by desert locusts causing damage to some pasture lands, increasing food prices, and chronic poverty. Up to 3.6 million adults and 150,000 children faced acute food shortage, hunger, and, in some cases, even starvation. Although it was severe, the food crisis did not come as a surprise to the authorities.

Nigerien mothers wait with their children at an emergency feeding center near Maradi.

In 2004, inadequate rainfall had resulted in a poor harvest that was mainly destroyed by waves of locusts. In certain areas, 100 percent of the harvest was destroyed. This caused a sharp rise—up to 20 percent—in food prices and other basic goods, which made the situation unbearable for many people who were already experiencing extreme hunger. Although the government offered subsidies, the impoverished farmers were still unable to afford to buy food for their families. The lack of food and water affected people as well as their animals, such as cattle, camels, sheep, and goats. The ill health and sometimes death of these animals, which in themselves are an important source of food, made the food crisis even more severe.

In February 2005, the United Nations established an emergency food program to help thousands of starving people, but sadly, international aid was slow and failed to reach many needy people. Hundreds of Nigeriens attempted to escape the food crisis by crossing over the border to Nigeria. Others marched in the capital of Niamey to demand free food. According to the World Health Organization (WHO), by mid-2005, an estimated 800,000 children under the age of five were suffering from a degree of malnutrition. Of these, at least 160,000 were malnourished and 32,000 were severely malnourished.

Today, children in Niger suffer malnutrition and disease because of severe poverty, continued environmental shocks, the high rate of population growth, and the increasing influx of refugees from civil strife in neighboring countries. The UN's 2018 Humanitarian Response Plan for the country estimated 1.4 million and 1.7 million people in Niger to be in need of food and nutrition support, respectively.

The addax may already be extinct in the wild.

of Threatened Species classifies the addax as one of the rarest and most endangered species in the world. Though they were once abundant throughout North Africa and the Western Sahara, there may be fewer than one hundred of these creatures remaining, mostly in the deserts of Niger. In fact, the only known self-sustaining population supposedly lives in the Termit Massif Reserve, a nature reserve in southeast Niger. That said, an extensive survey conducted in 2016 found only three individual animals, according to an alarming report by the IUCN.

This region is rich with other desert wildlife, including bustards and tortoises, gazelles, Barbary sheep, cheetahs, striped hyenas, fennecs, Rüppell's foxes, pale foxes, sand cats, wildcats, golden jackals, and vultures, just to name a few. Conservationists are working hard to ensure the survival of the addax in this unique and beautiful region. In the past, wildlife flourished in this isolated region. In recent years, however, the oil industry has encroached on the area and has begun to construct camps and airstrips. There are oil refineries and pipelines in the heart of this peaceful desert.

Apart from the threat from the oil industry, the wildlife population is also challenged by the practice of illegal poaching. In these parts, gazelle poaching is popular. One animal that is already extinct in Niger is the scimitar-horned oryx, which is a large antelope with long, backward-sweeping, curved horns. They were probably last seen in Niger in the 1990s. As late as the 1970s, there were several thousand of them, but today they are extinct in the wild. Their extinction was caused by the usual mixture of factors, including poaching, drought, desertification, and the destruction of their natural habitat by agriculture. It is possible, however, to see the scimitar-horned oryx in zoos across the world.

Niger's major national park is W National Park. The park was so named because the Niger River, which meanders through it, forms a letter "W."

W National Park was created in 1954 and declared a UNESCO World Heritage Site in 1996. (In 2017, the listing was expanded to include parts of Benin and Burkina Faso, and is now called the W-Arly-Pendjari Complex.) This national park covers a massive area of about 5,407 square miles (14,004 sq km), stretching across land in three countries: Niger, Benin, and Burkina Faso. Historically, the park has been inhabited by both humans and wildlife. The park is home to aardvarks, baboons, buffalo, caracals, cheetahs, elephants, hippopotami, leopards, lions, servals, and warthogs. Approximately 350 species of birds can be found here.

INTERNET LINKS

https://www.climatechangenews.com/2018/01/31/climate-change -affecting-stability-across-west-africa-sahel-un-security-council
This articles examines the effect of climate change and terrorism in the Sahel.

https://www.iucn.org/content/saharan-addax-antelope-faces -imminent-extinction
This article reports on the dire 2016 survey of the addax population.

https://www.iucnredlist.org/species/512/50180603
The IUCN Red List page for the addax is found on this site.

https://metamag.org/2017/10/18/french-state-owned-company -creates-ecocide-in-niger-to-fuel-its-nuclear-plants
This report looks at nuclear pollution in Niger.

https://whc.unesco.org/en/list/749
The World Heritage listing for the W National Park (now the W-Arly-Pendjari Complex) explains its value and includes images.

NIGERIENS

A man paddles a canoe on the Niger River near Niamey.

6

THE PEOPLE OF NIGER ARE MEMBERS of several ethnic groups, which correspond to the various languages spoken in the country. They are the Hausa, the Zarma-Songhai, the Tuareg, the Fulani, and the Kanuri. The Hausa make up about 53.1 percent of the population, while the Zarma-Songhai form 21.2 percent. The Tuareg people make up 11 percent, the Fulani 6.5 percent, and the Kanuri 5.9 percent. Smaller groups include the Gurma, the Tubu, and Arabs, each accounting for less than 1 percent. There are also several thousand French expatriates in Niger.

When the map of Niger and its administrative districts was drawn, the boundaries cut across traditional ethnic and linguistic regions. This had the effect of dividing certain related groups in some cases, and putting different peoples together in others.

Nevertheless, Nigeriens across the country are united by Islam—most are Sunni Muslims. And most Nigeriens use the Hausa language

Nigeriens are not Nigerians, though the people of both Niger and Nigeria share some of the same ethnicities. To avoid confusion, it's best to use the French pronunciation, "nee-zher-YEN" when saying "Nigeriens." The word Nigerians, on the other hand, coming from a British rather than a French colonial background, is said "nye-DJEER-ee-enz."

in trade and in everyday life. Many of the country's ethnic groups maintain close relationships with their relatives in neighboring countries such as Mali, Chad, and Nigeria.

THE HAUSA

The Hausa make up a little more than half of the Nigerien population. The traditional Hausa lands are divided between Niger and Nigeria. There are about 70 million Hausa people in Africa, with some 55 million in Nigeria and 10.5 million in Niger. Some of their ancestors can be traced back to the Sokoto Empire, an Islamic confederation that was based in northern Nigeria in the nineteenth century. The Hausa live in the mid-southern region of Niger, where the population density is the highest in the country. Their area extends past the city of Filingué in the west, Zinder in the east, and from Tahoua to Niger's border with Nigeria. A small number can also be found as far north as the Aïr region.

Although most Nigerien Hausa are farmers, they are also acknowledged as astute businesspeople. They have created an economy based on grain food

A Hausa village in the Bkonni part of Niger's Tahoua region shows the thatched round buildings common to rural Hausa settlements.

crops, livestock, cash crops such as peanuts and cotton, and craft production. There are many Hausa artisans in Niger, famous for their elaborate leatherwork. Because of mobility and extensive business contacts, the language of the Hausa is understood and widely spoken throughout the country. Despite a common language and distinctive cultural heritage, the Hausa ethnic group consists of numerous subgroups.

Muslim Hausa society is characterized by a complex system of rank based on profession, wealth, and birth. Occupational specializations are often passed down from father to son.

THE ZARMA-SONGHAI

The Zarma (sometimes spelled Djerma, or other variations) and the Songhai are different peoples who speak the same language. Because they share a common culture, other groups often view them as one ethnicity, but they consider themselves to be two separate people. They are distinguished from each other by a slight difference in their local dialects and the theory of their origins before the eighteenth century.

Forming about 21 percent of the total population, the Zarma-Songhai (also referred to as the Songhai-Zarma) are sedentary people who farm in the western part of the country near the Niger River. Apart from the late President Ibrahim Baré Maïnassara, the first Hausa president of Niger, political power has remained in the hands of the Zarma-Songhai since Niger's independence.

The Zarma population is twice as large as the Songhai. They mainly live on the left bank of the Niger River, around the city of Dosso. Other Zarma live in Mali and Benin. Although their origin is still a question, they are known for their fighting agility and have helped their cousins, the Songhai, in numerous battles against the Tuareg and the Fulani.

The Songhai live on the right bank of the Niger River and in the Ayorou-Tillabéri region on the left bank. They are primarily located in Mali and also live in Benin and Burkina Faso, as well as in the southwestern region of Niger. The Songhai are descendants of the fifteenth-century Songhai Empire.

THE TUAREG

The Tuareg are a large Berber ethnic group spread across the Sahara Desert regions of several nations in North and West Africa. They settled in the Aïr region as early as the seventh century CE, expanding their territory gradually to the entire Sahara region. Known as desert warriors, the Tuareg are famous for their fighting skills. Today, they are found in Algeria, Niger, Mali, and Libya.

In the past, the Tuareg operated the trans-Saharan caravan trade and were known to capture prisoners for trade or for use as slave laborers. Today, some Tuareg lead a nomadic life, although the droughts in the past decades have forced some to live permanently in cities such as Agadez.

The Tuareg are divided into three major subgroups: the Kel Aïr, the Kel Azawak, and the Kel Geres. The Kel Aïr live in the Aïr region and the Damergou region. Most of them are gardeners and shopkeepers. Most of the Kel Azawak are nomads, although a few animal herders can sometimes be found. The Kel Geres are herders and farmers.

Tuareg society, unlike most Muslim societies, is matrilineal, and women have a prominent role. In contrast to the women in many Arab and Muslim societies, Tuareg women are neither veiled nor secluded. Camp life is the Tuareg woman's domain, and she can own herds of animals and slaves. Women own the family property and manage the finances. They also play musical instruments and participate in organized musical performances.

The Tuareg men are sometimes called "blue men." Except for their eyes, they wrap their entire body in indigo-dyed clothes to protect themselves from the sandy winds and scorching sun, and the blue color rubs off onto their faces. At the end of the day, the men usually gather for their favorite pastime—the ceremonial sipping of tea next to a fire and talking about journeys in the desert.

THE FULANI

The nomadic Fulani (also called Fula or Peuhl) are scattered all over the Sahel and live in almost all parts of Niger, except in the northeast oases. There are more than two million of these people in Niger, and many more across West Africa, from Senegal to Chad.

A characteristic that sets Tuareg people apart from other Muslims is the veil. In Tuareg tradition, which is the opposite of Muslim tradition among most other people, the men wear the veil and the women don't. This headwear is one of the most important identifying features of this group and is an ancient custom dating back at least one thousand years. In fact, the Tuareg call themselves Kel Tagelmoust, or "people of the veil."

The veil is actually more of a turban, with an extension of fabric that wraps across the bottom of the face. The turban lies low on the forehead, and when the scarf fabric is in the highest position, it covers the nose and only the man's eyes can be seen. The entire headwrap, or veil, is made from one long piece of fabric.

Once a Tuareg boy enters puberty, he wears the veil in a family ceremony that marks his passage from adolescence to adulthood. From then on, he rarely goes unveiled, wearing the veil even while he is sleeping. The fold above the nose is frequently and slightly adjusted when he is in a group.

Although veiling is an ancient custom, its origins remain obscure. The veil holds an important place in Tuareg society because it is a symbolic manifestation of the role status plays in Tuareg groups: the lower the veil is worn, the higher one's status.

The close similarity of their language to the native language of Senegal indicates a possible origin in this West African country.

Most Fulani are engaged in agriculture, their traditional lifestyle. Others lead scholarly Islamic lifestyles, while the rest are nomads in the north. Migrations to urban or semi-urban regions have become more common in recent years due to unpredictable crop harvests. Although the Fulani are the fourth-largest group in Niger, forming about 6.5 percent of the total Nigerien population, they are not a majority in any region. The thiry-eight to forty million Fulani in West Africa constitute the second-largest ethnic group in the region, second only to the Hausa.

Within the Fulani, the Wodaabe form a distinct subgroup, holding tightly to their ancient traditions. Also referred to as the Mbororo or Bororo, they are nomadic, pastoral people who live in the Dakoro and Tânout region in the south. Most have preserved their animist beliefs, although some have converted to Islam.

As lovers of beauty, they hold an annual Gerewol (GER-e-wol) Festival, a beauty contest for unmarried men. Although Wodaabe women pay great attention to their appearance, it is mainly the Wodaabe men who embellish themselves. Popular accessories include earrings, coins woven into an elaborate hairstyle, bead necklaces, and multicolored charms.

Highly adorned Wodaabe men take part in the Gerewol Festival in 2017 in Agadez.

THE KANURI

Like other Nigerien ethnic groups, the traditional lands of the Kanuri people extend over national borders. Numbering about ten million in total, there are Kanuri populations in Niger, Nigeria, Chad, and northern Cameroon. They live mainly on the western side of Lake Chad, the site of the medieval Kanem-Bornu Empire.

Like the Hausa and the Zarma-Songhai, the Kanuri are primarily farmers. They also specialize in the preparation of salt, and many are excellent fishermen. Some are cattle herders. Through mixed marriages, they have blended with other groups. They have particularly close ties with Hausa speakers.

OTHER ETHNIC MINORITIES

Besides the main ethnic groups, there are a number of small groups who live in the Republic of Niger. Some of them work for the main groups, while others form their own settlements. Niger's minorities include the Arabs and the Gurma, who are pastoralists. The Arabs live north of Tahoua and Nguigmi, dress like the Tuareg, and speak their language, whereas the Gurma live in the southwest on the right bank of the Niger River. The other minorities consist of Africans from other countries and a small number of Europeans. A large proportion of Europeans are French, descendants of the French colonists.

INTERNET LINKS

https://kwekudee-tripdownmemorylane.blogspot.com/2014/02/ wodaabe-mbororo-people-nomadic-fulani.html
This site posts many beautiful portraits of Wodaabe people in Niger and several other West African nations.

https://www.pri.org/stories/2011-10-29/tuaregs-5-things-you -need-know
This is a brief overview of the Tuareg people.

LIFESTYLE

Nigerien village culture reflects the rural lifestyle of the Sahel region.

7

NIGER IS A COUNTRY OF VAST, WIDE open spaces. Great expanses of it, being harsh desert, support little or no life whatsoever. In the more habitable regions, there are some ten thousand villages, about half of which are tiny settlements with just a few hundred residents. In all of Niger, there are only four cities with more than one hundred thousand people—Niamey, Zinder, Maradi, and Agadez. Of those, only the capital, Niamey, has more than a million people—barely.

With more than 80 percent of Nigeriens living in nonurban areas, it's fair to say, then, that Niger is primarily a rural country. But that could change. While Niamey has a modern, cosmopolitan flair, it also has uncontrolled development and other problems typical of rapid urban growth. The same is true for Niger's other cities. Some demographers suggest that Niamey could explode to be the world's eighth-largest city, with forty-six million people by 2100.

Modernization is forcing people to adopt new lifestyles that are very different from those their parents and grandparents lived. Tuaregs, for example, have historically led nomadic lives for more than two thousand years, crisscrossing the Sahara Desert to trade merchandise such as beads, ceramics, glass, oil lamps, saffron, dates, nuts, flour, and salt. Today, however, many Tuareg people have found that lifestyle can no longer be sustained, and they have had to settle in one place. Many seek employment in the mining areas.

For now, however, Nigeriens still live mostly rural lifestyles determined by their location, ethnicity, occupations, and traditions. In the rural areas, no one works alone. To ensure survival, everyone has to chip in, in order to reap a bountiful harvest at the end of the agricultural year. The social hierarchy of past empires—nobles, free people, and descendants of slaves—still exists today. It contributes to the interactions of the groups and an individual's profession.

NOMADS

Nomads in Niger include mainly the Tuareg and the Fulani. The harsh and sometimes treacherous desert life requires strong ties between group members. To survive, everyone has to cooperate well and work together for the good of the group.

A Tuareg nomadic group usually consists of five noble families, five artisan families, and fifteen slave families. When several clans form an alliance, the name of the alliance is prefixed with the word *kel*. The largest Tuareg confederation is Kel Owey, which migrated to Niger around the fifteenth century. The leader of the clan is called *amrar* (AHM-rahr), which means "old." The leader decides on the daily tasks of the camp and allocates activities to the artisans and herders. When a confederation of several clans unites, their leader is called *amenokal* (ah-MEN-noh-kal).

Unlike the Tuareg groups, a less-structured hierarchy exists among the Fulani. When an individual is born, he or she is categorized, based on kinship, age, sex, and generation. These remain important determinants of existence, which the Fulani accept. Another factor that determines a person's status in Fulani society is the number of cattle the person owns and his or her success in rearing them.

Severe droughts in recent years have dealt a heavy blow to the nomads. They gradually lost most of their herds, and the remaining people were forced to take on a sedentary life for which they were not prepared. Many sought refuge in neighboring countries.

SOCIAL STRUCTURE

Niger's present population is the result of numerous migrations by different ethnic groups. Social structure generally originated in the days of the trade caravans and wars. Most of these rankings are also prevalent in West Africa. As a result, there is uniformity within the ethnic diversity of Niger. Each ethnic group is organized into family, clan, and confederations, and is well adapted to both sedentary and nomadic lifestyles.

For example, within the Tuareg community, several family groups make up a clan. A series of clans may unite together under a supreme chief, forming a kel

A Niamey mother kisses her children.

or confederation. (The word *kel* means "those of.") Tuaregs define themselves according to their specific kel. For instance, Kel Ahaggar are "Those of the Ahaggar Mountains."

Status is usually inherited. Nobles and warriors are at the top of Tuareg culture, and Islamic clerics, or *marabouts*, come next. Below them are free men, followed by casted groups such as blacksmiths and other occupations. Below all these are freed slaves. The lowest rung is reserved for slaves. All these free and casted groups can have slaves—even slaves themselves, if they have the financial means.

The basic unit of Nigerien social life is the family. Nigeriens define themselves in terms of their patrilineage, with all males and females descending from a single male ancestor. Leaders are usually chosen from the oldest men in a family, and their duties include partitioning and allocating plots of land, resolving conflicts, arranging marriages, and officiating at ceremonies. Family members frequently consult them, and their advice is usually followed. Leadership is commonly passed down from father to son. The elders, who are also the keepers of oral tradition, maintain social organizations that determine interactions between members of a social group, their social behavior, and interactions with other ethnic groups.

FAMILY

Within the Hausa, intricate kinship relations develop through the male line, providing mutual support among the members in both rural and urban areas. The elders of a family intervene in every aspect of family life, such as promoting and arranging marriages for their juniors to strengthen family ties. Nonworking Hausa women stay in the family compound and only venture outside for medical treatment and family ceremonies.

Strong family ties among the Songhai group are illustrated by their large families. Married sons live with their parents. The living compound is divided

In 2003, Niger outlawed slavery. That is not a typo. In 2003, Niger passed the first law in West Africa that criminalizes slavery. Under that law, anyone who sells or keeps people against their will can be punished with up to thirty years in prison. But law or no law, slavery continues openly and unabated in Niger.

The 2018 Global Slavery Index estimates there are about 133,000 enslaved people in Niger. Another source estimates as many as 800,000, while yet another says "a minimum" of 43,000. The wide difference in numbers may partly be due to various definitions of slavery. But the best reason is provided by a landmark 2004 report by the antislavery organizations Anti-Slavery International and Timidria.

The groups interviewed 11,000 enslaved Nigeriens. Based on the responses, the number of slaves in the country was projected to be 870,363. However, with no way to account for duplication and overlapping in the data, that figure is not definitive. What is clear, however, is that there are many thousands of enslaved people in Niger; that slavery is most prevalent in the regions of Agadez, Tahoua, and Tillabéri; and that it is practiced predominantly—but not exclusively—by the Tuareg and Fulani people.

The report concluded that there is, as yet, no way to know the true number of slaves in Niger. The Nigerien government has never tried to find out. Why? Slavery is such a deeply ingrained tradition across much of West Africa that the practice continues unquestioned. Slavery in Africa goes back thousands of years. Although some people are stolen and sold into slavery, most slaves are born into their status; they are slaves of inheritance. They are usually forced to work long hours for no money, are frequently beaten, and are fed little. Women and girls are frequently abused and have to bear their so-called masters' children. In turn, the children are also owned by the masters, who often sell the young children, thereby breaking up family units and ancestral lines.

More important than numbers, however, is the question of how to put an end to this system. It was the abovementioned survey—when the responses were made public—that pressured the Nigerien government to pass a law criminalizing slavery. However, that same government has been extremely lax in enforcing that law.

In 2008, Hadijatou Mani Koraou, who had escaped from slavery, sued the Republic of Niger, with the help of human rights groups, for failing to protect her. She was sold into slavery at the age of twelve, held against her will, and beaten and abused for years. The case was brought before the Economic Community of West African States (ECOWAS) Court of Justice. In a landmark decision, the court ruled against Niger, embarrassing the government by attracting international attention.

into a main room for the father, a room for each of his wives, and rooms for his sons and their families. While the men go to work, Songhai women do household chores, such as fetching water, preparing meals, cleaning the house, and looking after the children.

For the rural Tuareg, family life surrounds the tent or compound, which bears the name of the woman owning the tent. Tuareg women enjoy prestige in their society. When a girl marries, her elderly female relatives will give her a tent as her dowry. The tent becomes a powerful element in the couple's relationship, as the husband risks eviction from the tent when spousal disagreements occur. Tuareg society differs from other Muslim societies in its cultural practices and beliefs. Music, dancing, and private courtship conversations are part of their lives, as all of these are considered expressions of joy and life.

Ancient animist customs (the belief that spirits exist not just in humans but in every object, including animals and plants), coupled with Islamic traditions, continue to define the lives of the majority of the people. Rural lifestyles are now being affected by a rising number of people who are receiving basic

A Tuareg man sits outside his tent in the Zinder region.

education in schools. A greater number of people, especially the educated, are also attracted to the cities.

In urban areas, there are more nuclear families, as young married couples prefer to live by themselves. However, a lack of housing is a major problem for the rapidly increasing population. Therefore, living quarters often have to be shared with other family members, thus leading to overcrowding. With a rise in the number of homeless people, there are more thefts and social problems. Despite these deterrents, many young people still leave their villages for work opportunities as well as the convenience of the cities.

WOMEN IN SOCIETY

Many women in Niger live in a patriarchal system dominated by a conservative interpretation of Islam, which has contributed to the exclusion of women from full participation in political and social life. As in most West African countries, discrimination against girls in education also exists in Niger. The result is an incredibly low literacy rate of 11 percent among females. The literacy rate of males is also low, but more than twice that, at 27.3 percent.

Among the women who receive an education, only a few reach high levels of public administration. However, things are gradually changing for the better for women in Niger. Following the 2016 legislative election, for example, women made up 14.6 percent of the seats in the National Assembly. This demonstrates a vast improvement in the position of women in Nigerien society: after the 1995 elections, the legislature only had one female member. Today, women politicians hold some important portfolios in foreign affairs, enterprise privatization and redevelopment, employment and public works, and population and social action, to name a few.

In rural areas, women are actively involved in efforts to improve their children's health. Much of their time is spent hauling water, gathering firewood, doing the numerous household chores, and taking care of their offspring. Nigerien women have a high fertility rate, with an average of seven children each.

Many women's organizations are working in Niger to enhance the condition of women and their children. For example, UNICEF is working toward empowering women in the region of Maradi to improve child survival and tackle poverty. Representatives visit towns and villages to promote essential family practices such as simple ways to treat diarrhea. Other projects include sessions where mothers and women are taught about the importance of hand washing, complimentary feeding, vaccinations, and hygenic techniques of breastfeeding. Women are also taught how to ask for medical help or advice from health professionals for their children when needed.

In other parts of Niger, groups of women, with the help of women's organizations, are saving money to enable them to start their own small businesses to generate income for their families. Other women's groups working in Niger include the Niger Delta Women for Justice, which aims to support disadvantaged women, particularly those in rural areas and urban slums. The charity CARE also runs training for women's groups in Niger. For example, the charity has worked in the districts of Dosso, Tahoua, and Tillabéri, helping women grow the livestock sector by developing access to credit and training, as well as educating them on ways to market their animal products. All these types of programs help women become more involved and better equipped at caring for their family, which gives them a sense of dignity. To help women who have been victims of domestic abuse, groups such as SOS Children Villages Worldwide, a charity set up in 1993 by the Nigerien government for orphaned and abandoned children, and a consortium of other Nigerien NGOs are focusing on providing legal and medical assistance to women.

According to the international aid organization Save the Children, Niger is the worst place in the world for girls and women. Child marriage, adolescent motherhood, education, access to health care, and female representation in government are among the indicators that put Niger at the very bottom of the list. To evaluate girls' and women's rights and opportunities globally, reseachers analyzed 144 countries. The bottom twenty were all in sub-Saharan Africa.

MARRIAGE AND CHILDREN

Niger has the world's highest rate of child marriage. According to UNICEF, in 2017, some 28 percent of girls were married by the age of fifteen; 76 percent were married by age eighteen. Child marriage is most prevalent in Maradi, Tahoua, and Zinder. Girls as young as ten years old in some regions are married,

WOMEN IN A MALE-DOMINATED WORLD

In Niger, despite the constitution's provisions for women's rights, the deep-seated traditional belief that women should be subordinate to men results in discrimination in education, employment, and property rights. Women's inferior legal status is revealed, for example, in head of household status—a male head of household has certain legal rights, but divorced or widowed women, even with children, are not considered to be heads of households. Among more conservative Hausa and Fulani families, women are shut away at home, and some are only allowed to leave their homes if they are escorted by a male member of the family. Tradition among some ethnic groups from rural families allows girls as young as twelve to enter into marriage agreements.

Female genital mutilation, which has been illegal since 2003 and is widely condemned by international health experts as damaging to both physical and psychological health, is still practiced by several ethnic groups in some areas of the country. Domestic violence and physical abuse against women are common. Traditionally, it is often considered normal for a husband to beat his wife.

Human rights experts have reported that 70 percent of women admit that their husbands, fathers, and brothers regularly beat, rape, and humiliate them. Although violence against women is rampant, the subject remains taboo in Nigerien society. In 1999, even though the male-dominated government signed the United Nations Convention for the Elimination of Discrimination Against Women, it made sure that reservations were made on key articles to limit a married woman's right to choose her own place of residence and to divorce.

Girls sit in the shadow of a tree outside their school in Maradi.

and the child has no say in the matter. Child marriages are therefore forced marriages. In certain rural areas, the common belief is that it's best to marry off a daughter before she reaches puberty, to ensure her virginity at marriage and thereby uphold family honor. It is marriage, not education or professional achievement, which brings women any measure of respect in this society.

A child bride must drop out of school, putting an end to her education. Her job, then, for the rest of her life, will be to care for her husband and mother-in-law, in complete obedience. Giving birth at a very young age, which is a typical outcome of this tradition, often damages a young girl's body, which has not finished growing.

Perhaps not surprisingly, in 2012, Niger ranked last in the Save the Children Index as the worst place in the world to be a mother. Niger has the world's highest fertility rate, at 6.35 in 2018, meaning the average number of children born to a woman. It also has one of the highest infant mortality rates, the fifth-highest in 2018, at 79.4 deaths per 1,000 live births. Among children under the age of five, 31.7 percent were underweight in 2016, the sixth-highest percentage in the world. As in many sub-Saharan African countries, the percentage of women dying in childbirth is also very high—553 deaths per 100,000 live births in 2015. These dire statistics are aggravated by entrenched traditions such as child marriage but are primarily due to Niger's deep poverty, hunger, and poor access to health services.

Muslim Hausa and Songhai-Zarma men can have up to four wives. Hausa polygamists are usually rich businessmen or respected elders. Secondary wives are more likely to be child brides. Under the practice of *wahaya*, a man may purchase a fifth wife, usually between the ages of nine and fourteen, who then becomes a slave. The women in such arrangements are also called wahaya. Their sons are considered legitimate but their daughters are slaves. Although Niger outlawed the practice in 2005, it remains common.

Divorce is allowed, although it is discouraged. In most villages, parents arrange their daughter's marriage without her approval. Custom requires the man to pay a marriage gift to his future in-laws. Cases of arranged marriages between cousins often take place, and their failure causes rifts between family members.

The rural customs of Hausa groups require that the oldest son of a family be polygamous, bestowing honor, respect, and consideration to his parents. His first wife's parents will offer their other daughters—the wife's younger sisters—to be the man's second, third, or fourth wife. Today, young, educated individuals oppose forced or polygamous marriages.

Tuareg society, on the other hand, has different marriage traditions. Monogamy is the rule, but divorce is allowed. Tuareg parents do not arrange their children's marriages. Instead, playful courtship develops between young Tuareg boys and girls during community festivities.

EDUCATION

Niger's system of education follows that of its former ruler, France. Although education in Niger is free, only a small fraction of children attend schools. In rural areas, the distance to school is a major obstacle, and secondary schools in particular may be few and far between. There are two universities, the Abdou Moumouni University in the capital city of Niamey and the Islamic University of Niger in Say. Before attending elementary school, children usually attend a school where they learn the Islamic way of life and to recite the Quran, the Muslim holy book. In some religious schools, the object is to memorize and recite, rather than to read, the scripture.

Given their financial situation, many rural families do not send their children to school because they cannot afford to buy them stationery and books. In addition, some parents' groups view the establishment of schools with suspicion. As their children are taught a foreign language, parents are afraid that a social gap will be created between them, and that the school might "steal" their children from them. Thus they are not always enthusiastic about sending their children to school. Some even go so far as to hide children from government officials.

Statistics provide an overall picture of school enrollment by gender and level. In 2017, almost 70 percent of girls and 80 percent of boys were enrolled in primary school. That same year, almost 21 percent of girls and more than 28 percent of boys were enrolled in secondary school, and only 2.45 percent of females and 5.76 percent of males were enrolled in college-level education. Note that enrollment is not the same as attendance.

With recent education awareness campaigns targeted at the rural areas, parents are now reconsidering the option of sending their children to school. There has also been an important shift in the language used for primary instruction—from French to one of the four different languages that represent each major ethnic group. Many now realize the importance of education, as agricultural efforts have often been thwarted by changing weather conditions. Efforts are now being made to educate more rural children by establishing tent or hut schools. When the nomadic group moves, the school moves with them. Nomadic children are also being encouraged to attend schools through offers of hot meals. To help rural families further, the government has established elementary schools with room and board to house nomad children. One inconvenience of such boarding schools is the children's early separation from their parents. The children do not go home to visit during the school year.

Schooling is officially free and in principle compulsory for children between the ages of seven and fifteen. At the end of secondary education, students take

the baccalaureate exam, which determines whether they can attend college. Most of the teachers in elementary schools are Nigeriens, half of whom are apparently unqualified, whereas professors in high schools and the universities are often French educators, teachers from other African countries, or US Peace Corps volunteers. There are also private schools, which teach only in French. There also exist Quranic schools that specialize in the traditional teachings of Muslim theology, law, and Arabic history.

Although the government grants scholarships to university students in Niamey, most of them come from well-to-do families and so don't need the money. Although antagonistic relations may exist among various ethnic groups, students from the different ethnic backgrounds generally treat one another with respect. Job prospects for graduating students are poor, forcing them to complete their training in Europe or other African countries.

Girls and boys sit in a classroom at the Friendship Primary School in Zinder.

HEALTH

Sick people wait to be seen in a small hospital in Niamey.

Health-care facilities in Niger are inadequate, and about a quarter of the population does not have access to health services. There are only a small number of health providers to serve the rapidly increasing population. In 2008, there was one physician for every fifty thousand people. There is a shortage of staff, and it is hard to obtain certain types of medicines. There are government hospitals in Niamey, Maradi, Tahoua, Zinder, and other large cities, with smaller clinics in most towns. In Niamey, there are some private clinics, but only the well-off can afford to use them.

The main causes of death in Niger are illnesses caused by parasites, especially malaria. Niger falls within the African meningitis belt, with outbreaks taking place between the months of December and June.

The government's health program includes eradication of diseases in rural areas and health education. Children are given vaccinations against smallpox and measles. Diseases such as tuberculosis, malaria, trachoma, and leprosy remain endemic and continue to pose serious health problems. Major causes of the spread of these diseases include a lack of running water and sewage systems. To ease these health problems, some Nigeriens seek the help of local medicine men, who usually blame the illness on witchcraft and evil spirits. Some thirty-six thousand people in Niger are living with HIV/AIDS. The highly pathogenic H5N1 avian influenza has been found in Niger, although it does not pose a severe risk. Life expectancy at birth in 2018 for Nigeriens was 56.3 years, which is low but improving over previous years.

INTERNET LINKS

https://www.antislavery.org/wp-content/uploads/2017/01/full_english_slavery_in_niger.pdf
This document provides a wealth of information on the topic of slavery in Niger.

https://www.girlsnotbrides.org/child-marriage/niger
This organization works to end child marriage worldwide.

https://www.globalpartnership.org/country/niger
This organization under the World Bank works to improve education in Niger.

http://www.makeeverywomancount.org/index.php/countries/west-africa/niger
This site offers articles about women's rights in Niger and Africa in general.

https://www.nytimes.com/2019/01/06/reader-center/niger-divorce-women.html
This article takes a close look at women's rights and lives in Niger.

https://www.osac.gov/Pages/ContentReportDetails.aspx?cid=24228
This US State Department Overseas Security Advisory Council page details crime, violence, terrorism, and other dangers in Niger.

http://uis.unesco.org/country/NE
This UNESCO page provides up-to-date education statistics for Niger.

http://www.worldcourts.com/ecowasccj/eng/decisions/2008.10.27_Koraou_v_Niger.htm
This post is the judgment document of the 2008 landmark court case of *Hadijatou Mani Koraou v. the Republic of Niger*.

RELIGION

The Grand Mosque of Agadez is the tallest
mud-brick structure in the world.

8

ISLAM HAS PLAYED A VITAL ROLE IN uniting the ethnic mosaic of Niger. The religion itself is practiced in different ways. Certain fundamentalist sects promote a very strict interpretation, while others are more lenient. Some groups use religious teachings to try to gain power, sometimes leading to conflict. In places where fundamentalists have control, the people are forbidden to adopt Western ways. For example, the leaders may intimidate members of humanitarian organizations that try to provide health education to women.

Although the great majority of Nigeriens are Muslims, many remain attached to their ancestral animist customs and incorporate them into their religious beliefs and practices. A few groups, such as the Bororo Fulani and the Azna Hausa, practice only their ancient religions. Although Christian missions are scattered throughout the country, they have had little success in converting the people. Only a tiny percentage of the population is Christian.

More than 80 percent of the Nigerien population is made up of Sunni Muslims, and a small percentage is made up of Shia Muslims. The remaining Nigeriens are Christians or people who hold indigenous beliefs.

THE INTRODUCTION OF ISLAM

The Prophet Muhammad established Islam in 622 CE in Medina, in what is now Saudi Arabia. Although the Prophet died ten years later, his followers established a vast empire across the Middle East, North Africa, and parts of Europe.

One of the earliest Muslim groups settled in Kanem, on the Chad frontier, in 947 CE. By the eleventh century, other Muslim groups, as well as merchants, scholars, nomads, and craftsmen, had settled in the area. Trade relations soon developed between Kanem and the Muslim states of North Africa, bringing prosperity to the region. It also brought an influx of Muslim merchants, blacksmiths, and religious scholars. Leaders of local clans turned into powerful rulers and often sought the help of Muslim scholars to expand their rule to adjacent regions.

BASIC TENETS OF ISLAM

Islam means "to submit" in Arabic. A Muslim submits to the will of God, which was revealed through the prophets, including those recognized by Judaism and Christianity. For Muslims, the last of these prophets was Muhammad, to whom the Quran, the word of God, was revealed by the angel Gabriel in the seventh century CE. The Quran is the holy book of Islam.

The fundamental belief of Muslims as stated by the *shahadah* (SHAR-HAR-dah), the Islamic testimony of faith, is that "there is no god but God (Allah) and Muhammad is his Prophet." Muslims repeat this testimony sincerely during many rituals. They believe that the revelations of Muhammad complete the series of earlier biblical revelations received by Jews and Christians. In Islam, Jesus Christ is respected as one of the prophets, but no more than that. The true teachings of Allah, Muslims believe, are finally clarified in the revelations received by Muhammad, the greatest of the prophets.

Islam stands on five pillars: to witness that there is no God but Allah and that Muhammad is his Prophet; to perform the required prayers; to pay the *zakat* (ZAHR-cut), or charity dues; to fast during the month of Ramadan; and to perform the pilgrimage to Mecca (hajj). Whenever possible, men pray in congregation at the mosque under an imam, and on Friday they are obliged to do so. Women may also attend public worship at the mosque, where they are segregated from the men, although most frequently they pray in seclusion at home.

Initially, almsgiving was imposed on people by means of taxing their wealth proportionately, with the taxes subsequently distributed to the needy and to mosques. Now such giving is left up to the individual.

In remembrance of Allah's revealing his word, the Quran, to Muhammad, Muslims partake in a month-long, obligatory fast. During Ramadan, the ninth month of the Muslim calendar, Muslims abstain from eating, drinking, smoking, and other activities during the day. Only those who are ill or otherwise exempt do not have to abstain.

The Grand Mosque of Niamey features a minaret with 171 steps from bottom to top.

All Muslims are expected to make the hajj, a pilgrimage to the holy city of Mecca, at least once in their lives to take part in the activities and rituals there. These activities are held during the twelfth month of the lunar calendar.

ISLAM IN NIGER TODAY

Like other African nations, Niger sends Muslim pilgrims to Mecca, the Muslim holy site and birthplace of the Prophet Muhammad.

Niger's constitution separates religion and state. However, it does not stop government officials from taking part in public religious ceremonies. Some Muslim men confine their wives to their house compounds, but the majority of women do not wear the veil or the hijab, a piece of cloth covering their head and hair, as do many Muslim women, such as those in the Middle East. However, this may be changing, as more and more fundamentalist practices take hold across the country.

CHRISTIANITY

In Niger, less than 1 percent of the population is Christian. Christians are primarily found in urban areas, particularly Niamey. Many are Europeans and non-Nigerien Africans who live in Niger. The main Christian denominations are Roman Catholic and Protestant. Even though the former colonial ruler, France, is a mostly Catholic nation, Protestants greatly outnumber Catholics in Niger.

Early missionary work in West Africa from the fifteenth to the nineteenth centuries focused on the communities on the Atlantic coast and countries south of Niger. The first Catholic mission in Niger was established in 1931 by Bishop Francois Steinmetz of Upper Volta. In the 1940s, African Missions of Lyon, known as the Fathers of Lyon, started their work in the city of Zinder. Unlike the precolonial Muslim missionaries and rulers in Niger, who legitimized polygamy and traded slaves, Christian missionary workers insisted that Nigeriens become monogamous, that they eliminate superstition, and that slaves be freed. Christians focused their efforts on building religious schools and improving public health facilities and dispensaries to attract converts.

THE BORI CULT

Although the main religion is Islam, many Nigeriens still practice traditional cult rituals to seek relief from sicknesses or to explain unfortunate occurrences. These practices include the Yenendi (yay-NAN-dee), an ancient ritual to summon rain, sacrifices to appease or feed the gods, and sanctification of animals such as snakes, which followers believe look after the safety of their families and community as a whole.

The Bori (BOH-ree), meaning "spirit," is a spiritual cult of Niger that is practiced by a Hausa group called the Azna. The Azna are descendants of the Hausa who were chased out of the Aïr regions by the Tuareg and are one of the few groups who still retain their traditional rites.

The Bori ritual is a ceremony organized to call on the gods to intervene directly in worldly events and human affairs by possessing the body of an initiated woman or girl. Members of the cult include women from many roles in the rural society. They usually pray to the gods to drive away sickness and infertility.

The initiation rites are a monthly event. In the presence of the chiefs, *serkin* (SIR-kin) Bori, the women to be initiated are brought forward by the Bori queen, who is called *magajiya* (mah-GAH-jee-yah). The chiefs are the ones who officiate at the ceremony. The women start the ritual by dancing and continuing until they are in a frenzied trance. The ritual ends when the woman collapses on the ground, indicating that she is finally a Bori—and possessed by a spirit.

In areas such as Maradi and Niamey, the ritual was so widespread and the cult influence so strong that the political support of the Bori queens was much sought after in the early days of independence. The leadership of the Bori queens was instrumental in the creation of several women's organizations, such the Union of Nigerien Women.

INTERNET LINKS

https://www.globalsecurity.org/military/world/africa/ne-religion.htm
This article offers an in-depth look at the varieties of Islam in Niger, while questioning how modernization, fundamentalism, and terrorism will affect these practices.

https://www.usnews.com/news/best-countries/articles/2017-03-01/in-africa-fighting-radicalism-through-religion
A video accompanies this article which looks at how some Muslim religious leaders in Niger are teaching religious tolerance and trying to prevent youth from being radicalized.

https://www.worldatlas.com/articles/religious-beliefs-in-niger.html
This site give a quick overview of religion in Niger.

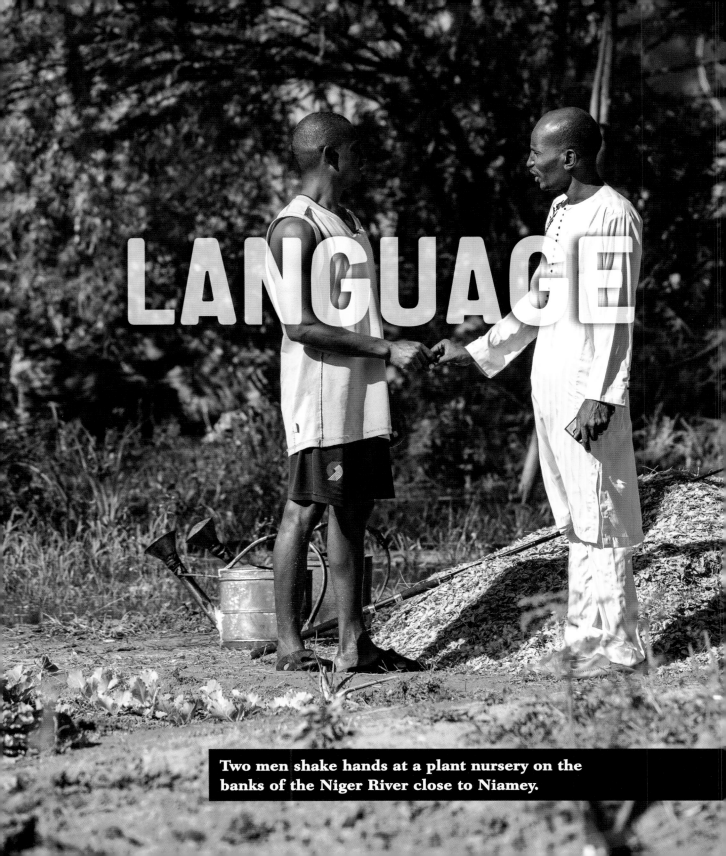

LANGUAGE

Two men shake hands at a plant nursery on the banks of the Niger River close to Niamey.

A COMMON LANGUAGE BINDS PEOPLE together perhaps more than anything else, even ethnicity. The languages of Niger came to the people through ancestral tradition, religion, and colonization. Language also divides people and is the primary element that separates Nigeriens into several different groups.

Nigeriens, especially in urban areas, generally speak two or three languages. Native languages such as Hausa allow for interactions within and between ethnic groups. The French language allows Nigeriens to conduct business and communicate with the rest of the world. Nigeriens also use Arabic to recite verses of the Quran.

Until France's occupation of the country, the main languages were Songhai, Hausa, and Tamasheq, and smaller communities continued to speak a variety of dialects. During the French occupation, a few schools that taught only French were built in the main cities, and the French-speaking people became an elite group.

Today, there are three major languages in Niger—French as the official language, Hausa, and Zarma (also called Djerma). The language of instruction in some schools and higher institutions is French, although recently primary schools have begun to teach in the main native languages of Hausa and Zarma. French remains the language used in the administration, industry, and finance. Most of the media, including television, radio broadcasts, and newspapers, use French. However, only a minority of the population speaks or reads French.

9

There are twenty-three individual, living languages in Niger. Of these, nineteen are indigenous and four are non-indigenous. Nine languages are designated as "vigorous," meaning they are in widespread use among all generations. Two are "in trouble," at risk of dying out as younger generations no longer use them regularly. The other languages have statuses that fall somewhere in between.

Vendredi le 1er juin 2012

Français
...ité 20   1ère séance

L'infirmier du village a reçu 850 comprimés 13
dont 500 de nivaquine. Les autres sont des
comprimés d'aspirine. Combien de comprimés
d'aspirine?

Solution   Opérations:

page 51   Combien de comprimés d'aspirine?

A child writes in French on the classroom chalkboard at the Friendship Primary School in Zinder.

There are twenty-three known languages and dialects in Niger, some of which are spoken by as few as three thousand individuals. Each ethnic group speaks its own language, but Hausa has become the language for trade in most of Niger. A number of French-Arabic schools, some of them financed by the fundamentalist movement in the major urban areas, conduct two-thirds of their lessons in Arabic.

HAUSA

Hausa is the native language of about half the Nigerien population. The language belongs to the Chadic branch of the Afro-Asiatic language family. In the regions where it is spoken, Hausa has a uniform vocabulary and structure that make its variations mutually comprehensible.

At the time of the colonial conquest, people began to use the Roman script as a written form of the Hausa language. The first documents in Romanized form dated from the early 1930s and were introduced by the British administration. The second writing system is called Ajami (ah-JAH-mee), which means "non-Arab" or "foreigner" in Arabic. Ajami uses the Arabic system of writing with minor adaptations for particular Hausa sounds. At the beginning of the nineteenth century, Ajami allowed learned, religious people to write Islamic poetry in praise of the Prophet Muhammad and his followers and to extol Islamic doctrine. Much of Hausa writing today, however, uses Romanized characters for transcription, similar to the Hausa literature printed in Nigeria.

ZARMA-SONGHAI

The language used by the Zarma-Songhai is the second most spoken native language. It is also used in Mali, northern Burkina Faso, and Benin. The Zarma language belongs to the Songhai family of languages in Mali, and the Songhai language belongs to the Nilo-Saharan group of the Afro-Asiatic family of languages. Although Zarma is a dialect of Songhai, the Songhai people of Niger understand Zarma. The differences between the two are subtle, and people who are not well versed in them can hardly tell them apart. When combined, about 21 percent of the population speaks the Zarma-Songhai language.

Zarma-Songhai and Hausa are considered the second languages of Niger. Other ethnic groups learn either Hausa or Zarma-Songhai, as required by their environment. These languages provide a tool of communication among the ethnic groups, including the Fulani, Tuareg, Kanuri, Tubu, Gurma, and other minorities, in markets and workplaces.

FULA

The language of the Fulani or Peuhl people is called Fula (also called Fulfuldé or Pulaar). It is classified as a Northern Atlantic branch of the Niger-Congo family of languages. It is spoken by about twenty-four million people spread across most of the countries of West and Central Africa. Despite the extremely large region they inhabit, their dialects only differ slightly.

Tifinagh script

The Tuareg alphabet is called Tifinagh.

The Fulani use two systems of transcription in their language—the Ajami, with slight modification for special Fula sounds, and Latin characters modified for special consonant sounds.

TAMASHEQ

The language of the Tuareg is Tamasheq, which has its own alphabet called Tifinagh (tee-FEE-nahr). Tamasheq is one of the Amazigh (ah-mah-ZEER) or Berber languages found in North Africa that belong to the Afro-Asiatic family. Because they are part of a matriarchal society, Tuareg women are responsible for passing on to their children their ancestors' language and its transcription. Women's duties include teaching the young the Tifinagh alphabet, which recently has become more popular with the advent of a strong movement to revive the Berber culture and language in Morocco and Algeria. Until recently, Tamasheq was limited to poetry and love messages. It is now used in more aspects of Tuareg life. During their uprising, the Tuareg demanded political autonomy and greater control of their cultural and linguistic heritage.

OTHER LANGUAGES

There are other languages and dialects used by the smaller ethnic groups. The Kanuri and the Tubu languages belong to the Nilo-Saharan family, while Gourmanchéma, the language of the Gurma, belongs to the Niger-Congo family. The Kanuri people in Niger use the Ajami transcription to write Kanuri. The Tubu language is spoken by the Tubu people, who also speak Arabic.

LANGUAGE AND THE STATE

During its occupation of Niger, France did not try to impose the French language on Nigeriens. Only a limited number of schools were built. After independence, despite the government's efforts to improve literacy, only one-fifth of Niger's population spoke fluent French. Beyond the urban areas, French is rarely spoken today.

Since independence, the Nigerien government has retained French as the official language, while actively promoting the native languages. The government has included news in the native languages in television broadcasts. The television station in Niger broadcasts daily news in Hausa and Zarma in between French programs, and it also broadcasts news in Tamasheq, Fula, Kanuri and Tubu, Gourmanchéma, and Arabic. The few radio stations in Niger also provide slots for news in the native languages.

During a national conference in July 1991, a proposal to make Hausa the official language of Niger failed as the other major ethnic groups opposed it, especially the politically powerful Zarma-Songhai and Tuareg groups. As a result, the government has decided not to have one definite language or fixed education program but to recognize the languages of the five major ethnic groups.

Nigeriens protest against the French mining company Areva. "*Trop c'est trop*" means "Enough is enough." The sign also says, "Clear out, Areva, colonization is over!"

THE MEDIA

The media in Niger are made up of state-funded media as well as privately owned independent media. Because the population is largely illiterate and dispersed over great distances, radio is the main way people access news, information, and entertainment. Wealthier people in the cities have televisions, but the rural population cannot afford the expense of owning a TV and often don't have access to electricity. Likewise, a mere 4.3 percent of the population uses the internet.

The Office of Radio and Television of Niger, or ORTN, is the state broadcaster of Niger. ORTN operates the Télé Sahel terrestrial television station, Radio Voix du Sahel ("Voice of the Sahel") radio network, and the TAL TV satellite station, which was formed in 2004. Ténéré TV is a private channel based in Niamey. Telestar, another channel operating from Niamey, is a pay-TV channel of Niger Television.

In addition to the ORTN national and regional radio services, there are privately owned radio networks that total more than one hundred stations. More popular radio stations include Anfani FM, Radio Sarounia, Radio et Musique, and Tenere FM. Nigeriens also have access to the BBC Hausa service and Radio France Internationale via satellite.

The government publishes a French-language daily newspaper, *Le Sahel*, and its weekend edition. There are approximately twelve private French-language weekly or monthly newspapers, some of which are affiliated loosely with political parties.

PRESS FREEDOM

In 1997 a press law was specifically introduced to control media criticism of the government. However, after the reinstallation of democracy in 1999, the media in Niger was allowed more freedom and independence. During the coups of 1996, 1999, and in the 2000s, free and private media were suspended, and many journalists were arrested and sometimes imprisoned. After the Tuareg uprising in 2007—2008, press freedom was severely curtailed. In 2010, that freedom "improved considerably" and media offenses were decriminalized after President Mamadou Tandja was ousted, according to Reporters Without Borders (RSF).

However, the atmosphere of journalistic freedom is deteriorating. In 2015, at least eleven journalists were arrested for covering a variety of sensitive topics, including the arrest of opposition leader Hama Amadou, the Boko Haram insurgency, and student demonstrations. Since that year, RSF has tracked a downward trend in press freedom as several respected Nigerien journalists have been jailed or deported by the government. In 2017, just to name one instance, the well-known TV news presenter Baba Alpha was arrested and jailed for one year and then deported to Mali for being "a threat to internal state security." Alpha was often critical of the government. In 2019, RFS ranked Niger 63rd in its annual World Press Freedom Index, a decline from its 2015 status at number 47.

INTERNET LINKS

https://www.ethnologue.com/country/ne/languages
This site provides an overview of the languages in Niger.

https://languagesgulper.com/eng/Hausa.html
This site offers an overview of the Hausa language.

https://www.omniglot.com/writing/zarma.htm
An introduction to the Zarma language is provided on this site.

https://rsf.org/en/niger
This is the Reporters Without Borders World Press Freedom Index page for Niger.

ARTS

Ancient rock art in the Nigerien desert depicts three large-headed figures.

A RT PLAYS AN IMPORTANT ROLE IN Niger's culture and economy. Artisans in each ethnic group excel in making one or two types of artifacts, depending on their living environment and way of life. Pottery making, particularly earthenware water jars, is the forte of Zarma women.

The Songhai make blankets and weave mats. Tuareg artisans make excellent silver jewelry with elaborate motifs and leatherwork with exquisite designs. They also sculpt wood and make utensils, tent equipment, and saddles. Fulani women are adept at engraving calabashes, weaving, and basketry. The Hausa produce some fine woven textiles, as well as exquisite, tightly woven baskets.

Although Nigerien arts have retained their traditional forms, modern Nigerien painters have drawn inspiration from Western and Muslim styles and integrated them in their work. For example, Rissa Ixa (b. 1946) is a Tuareg painter born in Ayorou. His paintings, in a manner reminiscent of folk art, are scenes of the vanishing Tuareg life. His goal is to preserve cultural heritage by educating society.

Exhibitions of Nigerien art are usually held in the National Museum of Niger in Niamey. Built in 1958, the museum exhibits many artifacts and works of art by the different ethnic groups.

10

Niger enjoys a vibrant traditional and contemporary arts scene and is well represented in the fields of dance, literature, storytelling, painting, theater, cinema, and music. Many artists use their work as a platform to provoke thought and discussion about Niger's social and political issues.

MUSIC AND THE TUAREG

Playing music and singing are important elements in any Nigerien social event. Music is used to celebrate human events, such as births, weddings, circumcisions, and religious holidays. The musicians and their audiences share in a creative performance to experience a communal activity and to express feelings of camaraderie.

A Tuareg woman plays an *imzad*, a traditional instrument made of a goatskin-covered gourd or wooden body. Played with a curved bow, it has a single horsehair string.

As guardians of traditions and customs in the Tuareg society, women have greatly contributed to the Tuareg cultural heritage. As a result, music is not a man's sole privilege; women play music as well, although their styles differ. Women play most traditional instruments, except flutes.

The women's musical styles include the *tindé* (TUHN-day) and the *ezelé* (ay-ZAY-lay). The tindé is the most common musical rhythm in Niger. It is created by a drumlike instrument called a tindé that is made with a mortar with goatskin stretched across its opening. In the tindé performance, the player also sings to the rhythm she makes with the instrument. Ezelé is a type of dance music played by women to accompany male dancers.

LEATHERWORK AND JEWELRY

Tuareg artisans, called *inadan* (EEN-ah-dan), are excellent craftspeople, making silver jewelry, saddles, camel bags, tools, utensils, talismans, and water containers from goatskins. They also specialize in leather products, such as traditional money purses and shoes. Leather shoes are made from rawhide for protection from scorpions, thorns, and sand fleas. The soles must be wide to allow support on the fine sand. Decorative patterns are intricate, and when dyed leather is used, these items become art pieces that can be worn only at special occasions. From the Saharan scrub and trees, artisans make ladles, bowls, and beds. Ladles are embroidered with dyed wool, apart from leather.

Tuareg artisans create a wide range of rings, anklets, and amulets. But the best-known jewelry item is the Agadez silver cross, called a *teneghelt* (te-NER-gelt), sometimes referred to as the Cross of the South (of Europe). Several designs exist, with each pattern representing a clan or confederation. In Niger, nearly every city is represented by its silver cross.

HAUSA FOLKLORE

Because of the nation's low literacy rate, Niger's folklore is best preserved in the form of oral tales, legends, and proverbs. Riddles, poetry, and the lyrics of old songs also contain some age-old stories. The literature of the Hausa people is vast and varied. As the Hausa converted to Islam, they also began to transcribe poetry in Ajami script. The main characters in a Hausa folk tale can be an animal, a man, a woman, a hero, or a villain. All folk tales attempt to highlight some traditional values and morals of their culture. Other tales include legends, which can be historical accounts of former rulers or stories of spirits. The Hausa believe in the presence of powerful spirits that intervene in their daily lives.

A silver pendant crafted in the form of the famous cross of **Agadez** is a popular jewelry item in **Niger**.

WALL DECORATION

To add sparkle to the earthy tones of their homes, the Hausa paint colorful motifs on the exterior walls. The patterns are often traditional Islamic and African styles. African motifs underline much of the decoration found in Hausa textile embroidery and wall decorations. Elaborate and intricate decorative patterns are also part of Hausa architecture. Early geometric mud decorations mainly adorned doors and other openings, and they were probably old charms to ward off evil intruders. Later the decoration expanded to include entire walls.

GRIOTS

Africa's oral traditions can be compared with the abundant libraries in Western countries. To retain this oral tradition, every ethnic group has griots, who are masters of the spoken word. During cultural celebrations in villages and cities, the eloquent griots will share with their audience many centuries-old folktales, stories, proverbs, poetry, legends, riddles, and historical epics. Their moving tales have captivated Western researchers interested in the cultural history of Niger and West Africa. These scholars have recently started to concentrate on learning more about the rich Nigerien customs and traditions, as well as their literature, history, sociology, and anthropology.

As a poet, storyteller, and musician, the griot is a walking encyclopedia for his people. He knows all the historical and cultural facts about his people, community, and country. He is the transmitter of a wealth of knowledge from one generation to another. Sometimes he is an official member of the royal court of a local chief, living permanently among his community. In some villages

A Hausa griot tells a story.

OUMAROU GANDA

Oumarou Ganda (1935–1981) was a Nigerien director and actor who introduced African cinema to an international audience in the 1960s and 1970s. Ganda was born in Niamey in 1935 and belonged to the Zarma ethnic group. He met French anthropologist and filmmaker Jean Rouch when he was living in Côte d'Ivoire, and Rouch introduced him to film and the cinema. Ganda played the lead role in Rouch's film, Moi un Noir *("I, a Negro") in 1958.*

When Ganda returned to Niamey, he became involved in the Franco-Nigerien Cultural Center. After receiving training in directing, camerawork https://rsf.org/en/niger , and sound, he became an assistant technician. Ganda's first autobiographical film, Cabascabo *(1968), based on his experiences in Indochina, was written in response to a screenplay competition organized by the center in 1968.*

His most famous film, Le Wazzou Polygame *(1970), won the first FESPACO (The Panafrican Film and Television Festival of Ouagadougou) Best Film Award. This film deals with polygamy and forced marriage and is critical of the powerful in Nigerien political society. His other films include* Saïtane *(1972) and* L'Exilé *(1980). Ganda also made documentaries. He died of a heart attack on January 1, 1981.*

After his death, as a way to honor Ganda and his work, a major cultural center, Le Centre Culturel Oumarou Ganda, was named after him. Another posthumous honor included the FESPACO African Feature Film Award, named the Oumarou Ganda Prize.

he lives apart from the local community but is allowed to speak freely. A griot can also be employed to work in a village or a city. He is hired for family celebrations and electoral campaigns. There are griots in all the Zarma-Songhai, Hausa, and Kanuri ethnic groups.

The griot is both feared and respected in Nigerien society. According to African wisdom, words are God's gift to a griot. They are considered sacred, and Nigeriens believe they contain magical powers that the griot can summon in ritual chants and rhythmic incantations to feed nature's spirits and forces. A griot may also extol the glories of powerful rulers or scoff at past incidents. Some griots have special relationships with their masters, acting as advisors.

In the past, during wars, the griots would accompany their masters, usually rulers of a region, to battlefields so that they could tell stories to boost the boldness and strength of the soldiers.

LITERATURE

Currently, Nigerien authors publish very few books in local languages. Until recent decades, the country's culture was conveyed orally from one generation to another. During family gatherings, the older folks would impart to the young their knowledge of the history and traditions of Niger and their ethnic group, as well as their own experiences.

As the African saying goes, "An old man who dies is a library that burns." Many Nigeriens are starting to realize the historical disconnection that can result from the lack of writing. This accounts for the increase in Nigerien literature in French that can be found today. The authors record the rich oral traditions and customs, giving the words of older generations an everlasting life-span.

The first Nigerien ever to publish a book before independence was Ibrahim Issa. He wrote *Les Grandes Eaux Noires* ("The Large Black Waters"). His most popular work is a book of poetry called *La Vie et Ses Faceties* (Life and Its Jokes), which contains the exploits of great African leaders, such as Samory, Issa Korombey, Béhanzin, and Lumumba. The book is written in the style of an African traveling poet and musician.

Another prominent writer was Boubou Hama, the former president of the National Assembly, who died in 1982. Born in 1906 he was the author of more than forty books, including important works on ancient empires, as well as traditional folktales and essays. In 1970, he was awarded the Grand Prix Littéraire de l'Afrique Noire, the great literary prize of sub-Saharan Africa, for his autobiography, *Kotia Nima*.

More contemporary writers include Oum Ramatou and Hélène Kaziende. Oum Ramatou is a writer born in Niamey in 1970. She wrote *Le Regard* and *Désiré*. Hélène Kaziendé was born in 1967 in Niger. She now lives in Togo. She is a teacher and a journalist. She published a novel, *Aydia*, in 2006. Her short

ALPHADI: AN AFRICAN FASHION DESIGNER IN PARIS

Born to a Tuareg father from Timbuktu in Mali and a Tuareg mother from Niger, Seidnaly Sidhamed Alphadi (b. 1957) is an important representative of new African fashion. He skillfully combines the colors and styles of Africa to attract Western taste. He is one of the few African fashion designers who has made a name for himself in the international fashion scene in Paris and New York.

Alphadi, which is the name he goes by, worked hard to become what he is today. While preparing for a doctorate in tourism from a school in Paris, he took evening classes in fashion and design and worked as a model for Giorgio Armani. On his return to Niger, he held the position of director of tourism promotion but resigned soon after. He headed for Paris and New York to complete his training in fashion design. In 1986, he introduced his first collection and has since won countless fashion prizes and medals. In 1987, the Federation Française de la Couture et du Prêt-à-Porter bestowed upon him the award of Best African Designer. Other awards include the Chevalier de l'Ordre de Mérite de la France in 2001 and the Kora Fashion Award–South Africa in 1999.

In 1999, Alphadi expanded his label to include a new sportswear line called Alphadi Bis. He also worked with well-known US jeans brand Wrangler to create Alphadi Jeans to appeal to a younger crowd. In 2000, he made history by launching l'Air d'Alphadi, the very first perfume by an African fashion designer.

More recently, in 2012, he created the Alphadi Foundation, with the aim of improving the living conditions of women and children in the Sahara. The designer was named a UNESCO Artist for Peace in 2016.

Niger's self-taught legendary musician Mamman Sani poses with his first and second albums in 2016 in Niamey.

story "Le Déserteur" ("The Deserter"), published in 1992, was awarded a prize at the literary competition organized by the radio station Africa No 1.

There are virtually no Nigerien literary works translated into English.

MODERN MUSIC AND ART

Contemporary art is embraced by younger Nigeriens. In Niamey, groups of young singers—for instance, the group Black-Daps—perform Nigerien rap music, using music to convey messages about social problems, such as drugs and AIDS. Newer music artists combine hip-hop elements with African music traditions, creating a unique sound. In more fundamentalist communities, however, such Western-influenced music would be discouraged.

The freelance theater company Les Tréteaux du Niger has been innovative. Instead of waiting for the public to attend plays, the freelance comedians decided to seek their audience wherever they may be. Their repertoire includes six original creations adapted from Molière, Corneille, and Shakespeare, and they have performed in towns and villages in Niger, other African nations, and Europe.

INTERNET LINKS

http://alma.matrix.msu.edu/the-language-of-african-music -zarma-songhai
This site provides extraordinary videos of Nigerien traditional music artists.

https://wellsbringhope.org/niamey-capital-of-niger-and-the-next -fashion-capital-of-the-world
This charitable organization focuses on Niger, and on this page it highlights fashion design in Niamey.

https://wellsbringhope.org/nigerien-hip-hop-the-voice-of -nigers-youth
This page gives a brief overview of hip-hop music in Niger.

LEISURE

Nigerien jockeys compete during a horse race
in 2016 at the hippodrome of Niamey.

11

NIGERIENS ARE A VERY SOCIABLE people. They enjoy taking part in festive gatherings, such as weddings and birth ceremonies. Communal gathering places, including markets, are not only a place for daily grocery shopping but are also busy and lively arenas where, among other things, friends meet and spread the latest news and fashion trends.

Besides traditional activities, modern sports, such as soccer—called football outside of the United States—have caught on in Niger. Many people now enjoy watching matches either live or on television. City dwellers enjoy going to the movies.

SPORTS

Horse racing and camel racing are sports with deep roots in Nigerien culture. But traditional wrestling, or sorro wrestling, is the "king of sports," not only in Niger but throughout West Africa.

Among modern sports, soccer is the preferred sport of Nigeriens, offering a source of entertainment for men and young boys. Rugby and martial arts are also important competitive activities. But soccer has become the most popular modern sport in Niger because of the bonding that results from the various African and World Cup competitions that

Traditional wrestling promotes unity among the Nigerien people. Cultural elements imbue the sport with ancestral symbolism. The opening prayer (*fatiah*), praise poems (*take*), poems of self-praise (*kirari*), formal salutations (*gaysuwa*), the giving of gifts and gratuities (*kari*), and the wearing of charms (*gris-gris*) all heighten the magnitude of the championship events.

Children play football (soccer) in the streets of a poor neighborhood in Niamey.

attract millions of spectators. With a soccer league that organizes tournaments for teams from different regions, Niger is able to participate with other African countries on a regular basis.

The Nigerien government takes an active role in the promotion of sports in the country. So far, it has supported sports organizations and organized games, promoted traditional sports, and formed teams to take part in international games. In 2005, Niger hosted the fifth Francophone Games, which included track and field events, basketball, boxing, soccer, judo, table tennis, and traditional wrestling. In 2015, it hosted the Traditional African Wrestling Championship, in which Niger won the top team prize.

TRADITIONAL WRESTLING

The sport dates back thousands of years to a time when villages sent their best fighters to compete against each other, to measure each village's power and to provide entertainment. Today, each of Niger's eight regions sends ten fighters to the national competition, which has team and individual events.

Nigerien wrestling is somewhat different from the common forms of wrestling. It is more a mix of Japanese sumo wrestling and Greco-Roman wrestling. It is a stand-up form of grappling in which the object is to force one's opponent to the ground. The winner may not always be the heaviest or strongest. Besides physical training, preparation for the wrestling championship might include psychological exercises, animist rituals, and prayers. The sport is also practiced across West Africa.

In this sport, two fighters wearing lambskin loincloths compete on a surface of loose desert sand. The ring is a circle about 65 feet (20 meters) wide, surrounded by sandbags. During championship games, wrestlers parade in the arena, showing their muscles, while musicians entertain the spectators and camel riders perform dances. During the match itself, the first man to fall, or touch some part of his body to the ground—other than his feet—loses the fight. There are few rules, although punching, biting, and grabbing the loincloth are prohibited. Some athletes try to boost their chances by wearing magical amulets for good luck. They may also have a griot (traditional African poet) singing their praises on the sidelines as well as a personal shaman invoking spells.

To win the championship, the wrestler must win seven rounds. The winner is awarded a saber, a horse with a harness, a traditional turban and tunic, and a check that he receives from the hands of the Nigerien minister of youth and sports. In the 2013 national tournament, the Nigerien government also gave each participating wrestler two sacks of rice and two sacks of millet. International competition now takes place during the Jeux de la Francophonie and the Championship of African Lutte Traditionnelle, which was established in 1996.

More recently, Niger hosted the Africa U-20 Cup of Nations in February 2019. This youth soccer championship is organized by the Confederation of African Football (CAG) for players age twenty and below. Eight teams played in two host cities, Niamey and Maradi. Niger's team didn't win any games, but it was its first time appearing in this tournament. Mali won the series and earned its first title.

ENTERTAINMENT

Every large city has an outdoor cinema where Nigeriens can enjoy the latest movies. In Niamey, movie festivals, conferences, and art shows are held at the Oumarou Ganda Cultural Center or the French Cultural Center.

Household electronic equipment has brought dramatic changes to Nigerien leisure. Some of the wealthier urban dwellers own computers and other digital electronics. Many more own televisions and radios. American and other foreign TV shows are broadcast on Nigerien television and are very popular. Urban teenagers also enjoy watching Hindi dramas and action movies.

However, the majority of Nigerien people cannot afford such luxuries. Mobile-phone density remains low, at about forty-six cell phone per one hundred persons.

DARA

Both young and old men play *dara* (da-RAH), a game similar to checkers. There are usually two players. Pits of the dum-dum tree fruit are used as pieces. To play, rows and columns of holes are made in the sand. One player puts the pits in his share of holes, while his adversary uses small millet twigs in his holes. The objective is for each player to move his pieces to the farthest row of holes.

SHARRO

Sharro (SHAR-raw), or *sharo*, is a sportlike activity practiced by nomadic Fulani boys when they enter manhood. Sharro means "flogging," and that's exactly what it is—a beating in the form of a rite of passage, a test of endurance and bravery. It's performed by two opponents. According to his partner's age and category, the giver violently hits his partner with a tree twig or a stick a certain number of times. His partner, the receiver, must endure the pain, pretending not to be hurt. He must also smile at the audience to prove his excellent control over pain. A year later, the roles are reversed. The competition can continue for many years.

In festivals, the bare-chested competitors are escorted to the ring by young, unmarried women. Drumming heightens the sense of drama and excitement as the spectators cheer. A young man knows that if he breaks down, unable to endure the beating, he will be a disgrace to his family. If, on the other hand, he tolerates the pain without wincing, he will earn his manhood with pride.

Although this ritual is performed as a passage to manhood, older men also like to take part in it as a sport. But because this tradition is such a dangerous activity that has left people badly injured, the Nigerien government has banned it. Although the competition is no longer performed at public festivals and ceremonies in the towns, it goes on in less conspicuous locations.

INTERNET LINKS

https://www.aljazeera.com/news/2018/01/niger-wrestlers-face
-championship-event-180108183429068.html
This site offers an informative video about Niger's traditional wrestling championships.

https://www.voanews.com/a/a-13-a-2004-01-30-39-west
-66865232/260069.html
This is another article about traditional wrestling.

FESTIVALS

Muslims perform the Eid al-Adha prayer
in Niamey on August 22, 2017.

12

W ITH THE GREAT MAJORITY OF Nigeriens being Muslim, the Islamic religious observances dominate the year in Niger. However, secular, state, and traditional festivals mark the passing of the year as well.

SECULAR AND STATE HOLIDAYS

January 1, New Year's Day, is a public holiday. However, because most Nigeriens are Muslims and celebrate only the Muslim New Year, the secular New Year is just a welcome day off for most working people. Labor Day (May 1) and Concord Day (April 24) are also national holidays. Concord Day celebrates past peace accords with Tuareg separatist groups, but also, more generally, peace, cross-cultural tolerance, and social justice.

Leftover from the days of French domination, Christmas and Easter Monday are also public holidays. These are religious holidays for Christians, but for the majority of Nigeriens, they are simply secular days off.

The patriotic holidays are Nigerien Independence Day (August 3) and Republic Day (December 18), which is the republic's birthday.

MUSLIM HOLIDAYS

Muslim religious observances follow the lunar calendar, so they are held on different dates every year. The most important ones are observed as public holidays in Niger.

Concerns about terrorism have kept tourists away from the Sahara and Sahel regions of Niger. Ironically, without tourism to support the barebones economies in those areas, local authorities worry that discouraged young people will fall prey to extremist groups. With such colorful extravaganzas as the Aïr Festival in Iférouane, they hope to lure tourists to return.

Annual Muslim sacred observances follow the Islamic calendar, which is different from the Gregorian, or Western, calendar. Where the Gregorian calendar marks the years beginning from the time of Jesus Christ, the Islamic era begins with Muhammad's flight from Mecca to Medina in 622 CE. This journey is known as the Hegira, so Islamic dates are preceded by AH, or anno Hegirae, ("the year of the Hegira"), rather than AD, meaning anno Domini ("the year of the Lord") in Latin. This book uses the abbreviation CE, designating "Common Era," which, like anno Domini, begins on the year of Christ's birth.

Unlike the Gregorian calendar, the Islamic calendar is based on the lunar year, which has twelve months but only 354 days. The Islamic year, therefore, is generally about eleven days shorter than the Gregorian year. The twelve months of the Islamic calendar are:

1. *Muharram*
2. *Safar*
3. *Rabi al-Awwal*
4. *Rabi al-Thani*
5. *Jumada al-Awwal*
6. *Jumada al-Thani*
7. *Rajab*
8. *Shaban*
9. *Ramadan*
10. *Shawwal*
11. *Dhu al-Qidah*
12. *Dhu al-Hijja*

MUHARRAM   The first day of Muharram, the first month of the Islamic lunar calendar, is celebrated as New Year's Day, also called Muharram. Like the secular New Year's Day on January 1, it is a public holiday. But because of the lunar calendar, the day rotates through the seasons and falls on a different day each year.

MAWLID AN-NABI Known in French as Mouloud, this day is the Prophet Muhammad's birthday. It is celebrated on the twelfth day of Rabi al-Awwal, the third month in the Islamic calendar. It was not observed until the ninth century of Islam, when its exact date was determined. On this day of special prayer, men journey to the main mosque to hear stories of Muhammad's life told by the imam, or religious leader. Women usually gather at a friend's home for their own prayers.

RAMADAN The month of fasting is signaled by the sighting of the new moon. All healthy adults are expected to fast through the month of Ramadan. Fasting requires Muslims to abstain from food, drink, and smoking between sunrise and sunset. This encourages a time of introspection and prayer. As the month of Ramadan draws to a close, Muslims gather to watch for the new moon. When that appears, there is great rejoicing, for the month of fasting is over and the festival of Eid al-Fitr (Id ul-FIT-r) can begin.

LAILAT AL-QADR Also known as Shab-e-Qadr, Night of Decree, Night of Power, or Night of Measures, this holiest of occasions celebrates the night Muhammad received the first verses of the Quran. It occurs on the twenty-seventh day of Ramadan. In Niger, it is an official public holiday and day off.

EID AL-FITR Also called the Feast of Eating, this festival marks the end of Ramadan and is celebrated with family and friends. On this day, the men wake up early in the morning to gather in the mosque for prayers. After prayers, relatives and friends visit one another, and children are given money and treats. A large feast is served for lunch.

EID AL-ADHA This holiday, the Feast of the Sacrifice, is known in Niger as Tabaski. It commemorates the Prophet Abraham's willingness to sacrifice his son and is the highlight for those who have completed the hajj. The hajj is a pilgrimage to the holy city of Mecca in Saudi Arabia.

For male Muslims, Eid al-Adha starts with a morning prayer, led by an imam, or Muslim spiritual leader, at the mosque. At the end of the prayers, the imam will slaughter a ram, a signal to the followers that they can go ahead and slaughter their own rams. The sacrifice of a ram symbolizes giving oneself to Allah. The meat is usually distributed to friends, neighbors, and poor people. During this time Muslims are reminded to be compassionate and help the poor and needy.

THE BIANOU FESTIVAL

To celebrate the Muslim New Year, the Bianou festival is held in the city of Agadez to commemorate the birth of the Prophet Muhammad and the mysterious construction of the Great Mosque of Agadez. It is celebrated for three days and starts with *ettebel* (ET-bel), a drumming and a call from the minaret. As crowds gather, the ettebel players appear, followed by Tuareg dancers who perform spinning dances in their long, blue robes.

Agadez has been a sultanate since 1449, and the festival is held in the sultan's palace. Tuareg people from neighboring cities come to take part in the grand camel race, which includes more than two hundred traditionally dressed Tuaregs riding camels. To start the camel race, women musicians play tindé. The race begins outside the city, and the finish line is the courtyard at the sultan's palace. In the evening, crowds gather to listen to a *takamba* (TAH-kahm-ba) performance, music played by a traditional guitar player. Women start to gather in a circle, and the men start dancing. The women then join them in the dance.

SALT CURE FESTIVAL

Every fall, the Bororo Fulani and the Tuareg nomads gather after completing a yearlong seasonal migration and hold the Cure Salée (Salt Cure) Festival in In-Gall and Teguidda-n-Tessoum, where green pastures are abundant. In-Gall is located in an oasis with palm groves and date plantations. The name "salt cure" comes from the salt that is contained in the new grass, which is an essential part of the animals' diet. The nomads believe that the salt cure fattens the animals.

GEREWOL: A MALE BEAUTY CONTEST

As part of the Salt Cure Festival, the Wodaabe tribe holds an annual beauty contest known as the Gerewol. This contest, however, is not for women. Only men are allowed to participate, while women act as the judges.

After spending many hours decorating themselves with their most beautiful clothes and jewelry, the men line up to perform a dance. The participants, who have decorated their faces with pale yellow or bright red powder and painted the edges of their eyes with black kohl, are a remarkable sight. They dance forward, gracefully shifting and lifting their weight from one foot to the other while clapping their hands and singing. As they dance, they smile at a group of young unmarried women who are the judges.

It is customary for the dancers to keep their eyes wide open to emphasize their facial beauty, but their enormous eyes also evoke an astonished, otherworldly look. After the dance, the judges mix with the young men and choose the most beautiful. However, if the men are displeased with the judges' decision, fights can break out. The Nigerien government has attempted to stop this celebration because it often ends in violence.

Wodaabe men line up to perform in the Gerewol Festival.

Tuaregs on camelback take part in the Cure Salée (Salt Cure), or Festival of the Nomads, in In-Gall, northern Niger.

During the festival, the Tuareg, dressed in traditional clothes, hold camel races, and artisans exhibit their exquisite leather and wooden artifacts and jewelry. To offer support, the government regularly takes part in the celebration by distributing sugar, millet, and tea to the nomads. To kick off the celebrations, Tuareg women play tindé, a traditional Tuareg musical instrument, and sing. While they perform, the men proudly ride their camels around the racing grounds.

OTHER FESTIVALS

There are other traditional and colorful festivals in Niger that take place throughout the year. Yenendi is the rain feast, a purification ceremony in which rural Nigeriens request that the earth be showered with rain before the fields are planted. It is usually performed when there is a drought. The ceremony is called for by the village spokesman, who invites the villagers to gather around a sacred place outside the village, usually under a big gao tree. All the villagers join in the procession, dancing and singing while waiting for the rain to come.

Hotungo is the annual celebration of the cattle breeders held in Bangui. Wassankara is a political comedy festival held in certain areas of Niger. Children imitate politicians and local authorities. Hawan Kaho literally means "riding the horns." Traditionally, Nigerien butchers and their sons stage a sort of bullfight without weapons. They try to get hold of the horns of an angry bull and ride it. This festival is organized at the end of Ramadan and attracts thousands of spectators as well as tourists.

INTERNET LINKS

http://afrotourism.com/travelogue/gerewol-festivalniger-a-male -beauty-contest
This travel site includes an article with photos about the Gerewol Festival.

https://www.timeanddate.com/holidays/niger
This calendar site lists up-to-date yearly holiday observances for Niger.

FOOD

A Tuareg host pours tea for his guest.

13

NIGERIEN FOOD AND DRINK IS similar to that found throughout West Africa. The diet is commonly based on starchy carbohydrates, including grains such as millet, rice, sorghum, and maize; tuberous roots, including cassava and sweet potatoes; and beans. Spices such as saffron, nutmeg, cinnamon, ginger, and cloves are typical flavors. These spices were introduced into the cooking and foods of Niger by trans-Saharan traders.

In Niamey and other large cities, the French influence can still be found. French-owned stores carry food products, such as yogurt and ice cream, imported from Europe. Crusty baguettes take the place of the more indigenous African flatbreads. Because these products are very expensive, few Nigeriens can afford to enjoy them.

STAPLES

Millet is Niger's main staple. The traditional midday meal is *fura* (FOO-rah), a millet porridge prepared with water or milk, spices, and cooked flour. The pastoral Fulani rely on dairy products, such as yogurt, milk, and butter, but they also eat millet, sorghum, and corn porridge. Besides

Drinking tea is a highly ritualized occasion, always involving three servings. The same tea leaves are used for each round, and increasing amounts of sugar added, resulting in progressively weaker, sweeter tea. The first serving is said to be "bitter as death"; the second serving is "mild as life"; and the third serving is "sweet as love."

Millet has been cultivated in Africa for thousands of years. The fast-growing grass, native to West Africa, thrives in warm regions with poor soils. There are numerous kinds of millet worldwide, but the most popular is pearl millet, the type grown in Niger. The grassy plant produces small grains that cannot be eaten raw but can be cooked or processed into flour.

Millet is one of the most important staples in the Nigerien diet, making up more than 65 percent of the daily caloric intake. In rural areas, families will typically eat millet at every meal. It can be made into porridge or a thin soup, sweetened with sugar and spices, and served with goat or camel milk. It can also be served as a thickened starchy base for a savory stew or sauce.

millet, the Hausa diet also consists of sorghum and corn. The Tuareg nomads eat mainly grains. Dairy products, such as milk and cheese, and fruits, such as dates and melons, provide additional nutrition.

MEAT AND VEGETABLES

Fresh fruits and vegetables are expensive, and meat, eggs, and fish are only prepared during family celebrations and holidays. Fresh or dried vegetables, such as okra, onions, peppers, spinach, tomatoes, squash, pumpkins, eggplant, sorrel, and baobab leaves, are added to sauces or porridge. Mangoes, dates, and melons are usually consumed in large quantities when they are in season.

Fish is a favorite among the people who live near the Niger River and Lake Chad. Nigeriens enjoy snacks prepared with meat and grilled tripe, and cakes made with fried beans or peanuts. In markets, grilled mutton (lamb) brochettes are popular snacks.

For Muslims, Islam forbids the consumption of pork and alcohol. The meat also has to be fresh, and the animal must be slaughtered in accordance with Islamic principles.

An outdoor vendor grills meat at a food stand in Niamey.

TYPICAL MEALS

Nigeriens' typical meals consist largely of porridge, pancakes, or pastes made from millet flour. They eat pancakes at breakfast, porridge at noon, and pastes topped with other ingredients and sauces in the evening. Those who have access to fresh vegetables will often begin a meal with a colorful salad.

A normal midday meal in a rural or poor urban family consists of boiled millet or sorghum and buttermilk. Sometimes spices or sugar are added. In the evening, *tô* (TOH), a popular West African dish made with white millet or sorghum balls, is eaten with different kinds of sauces. The sauces are made from leafy greens, onions, tomatoes, dried legumes, spices, and meat, if there is any. If there is chicken, dried beans and sorghum usually complement the dish. In the rice-planting region along the Niger River, rice is eaten with local spices and spinach-like herbs and groundnuts. Dishes with smoked or dried fish are cooked with local ingredients. Most rural families have two meals a day. For the poorer ones, one meal per day is common.

In urban areas, wealthy families lead a more Westernized lifestyle. They also have the opportunity to try Western food. For them, a meal may consist of plenty of rice prepared with a tasty vegetable sauce and eaten with meat or fish. In contrast to the rural people, urban families can afford to have three meals a day.

The eating habits of the nomads in Niger are similar to those of the farmers. The main difference is that, compared with their fellow countrymen, they consume more milk and dairy products, such as butter. The dairy products are produced from cow's milk, which is also used to trade for grains. The nomads also eat a substantial amount of meat because, from time to time, they slaughter some animals from their herds.

SIPPING TEA

In many Muslim countries in Africa, a traditional custom is to drink hot and foamy tea, usually green tea with mint. For Tuaregs, tea drinking is a solemn affair in which each step of the preparation is carried out with care. Three cups are offered and consumed. The Tuareg say the first cup of tea is strong, the second cup is soft, which means it is slightly weaker than the first, and the third cup is light and is usually offered to the children.

In addition to its stimulant properties, tea offers drinkers an opportunity to hold long conversations, especially near a campfire while enjoying the starry desert night. To make tea, two pots are used. The steaming tea is poured from one pot to the other so that foam appears.

DRINKS

Tea is the most popular drink for Nigeriens. However, during special ceremonies and on journeys, the Tuareg drink *egherdjira* (ER-er-jee-rah), a drink prepared with pounded millet, dates, milk, and goat cheese. It is very rich and is sipped from a ladle.

In the cities, people sip strong, hot coffee for breakfast. Sometimes the coffee is mixed with milk. Soft drinks, found at every food outlet, are popular. They include Coca-Cola, Sprite, Fanta, and local soft drinks. People throughout Niger, and West Africa in general, also enjoy a drink made from hibiscus flowers called *bissap*.

In the villages, a local alcoholic drink, *bourkoutou* (BOOR-koo-too), made by fermenting millet, is very strong and is favored by the Hausa.

INTERNET LINKS

https://www.businessinsider.in/Niger-is-the-most-amazing -country-I-never-expected-to-visit/Even-if-you-never-make-it -to-Niger-the-countrys-a-reminder-that-there-are-interesting -and-unexpected-things-everywhere-and-that-any-country-no -matter-how-obscure-it-may-seem-can-be-its-own-adventure-/ slideshow/49433915.cms
This interesting travelogue is mostly photographs of the country but includes a few looks at dining opportunities.

https://www.worldtravelguide.net/guides/africa/niger/food -and-drink
This travel site lists some typical dishes from Niger.

DJERMA STEW

Often called the national dish of Niger, the stew can be made with or without meat.

Salt and pepper, to taste
1 chicken, about 3.5 pounds
  (1.5 kilograms), cut into parts
¼ cup (60 milliliters) vegetable oil
2 medium onions, sliced
1–2 cloves garlic, minced
1 tablespoon paprika (smoked or regular)
5–6 Roma tomatoes, chopped
1 teaspoon dried thyme
¼ tsp curry powder
1 bay leaf
2 cups (475 mL) chicken broth
2–3 carrots, peeled and sliced
¼ cup (5 grams) chopped fresh parsley
2 scallions, sliced
3 Tbsp peanut butter

Season the chicken with salt and pepper, then set aside. In a blender or food processor, combine the fresh tomatoes, onions, and garlic. Blend until smooth. Set aside.

In a large Dutch oven, heat the oil and add the chicken. Fry the chicken until brown on all sides. Add the blended tomato sauce to the chicken. Add the paprika, curry powder, and bay leaf and stir well. Add chicken broth, heat to a boil, then reduce to a simmer. Cover and cook the chicken for about 30 minutes or until tender. Remove a cup of liquid from the stew and whisk with the peanut butter in a separate bowl. Set aside. Add the carrots to the pot and cook for another ten minutes, or until they are tender. Pour the peanut butter mixture into the pot and stir. Allow the stew to simmer until thick. Adjust the seasoning to taste. Add the parsley and scallions, and remove the bay leaf.

Serve the stew over rice.

BISSAP JUICE

2 quarts water (about 2 liters)

2 cups (60 g) dried red hibiscus flowers (hibiscus tea)

2 cups (400 g) sugar

Fresh mint leaves, a few sprigs

2 teaspoons vanilla

2 cups (475 mL) pineapple juice (optional)

Bring the water to a boil. Remove from heat and add the hibiscus and mint sprigs. Steep for at least 10 minutes. Strain the tea into a pitcher. Add the sugar, vanilla, and pineapple juice, if using. Let cool.

It is usually served as a cold beverage, but hibiscus tea can also be served hot with sugar.

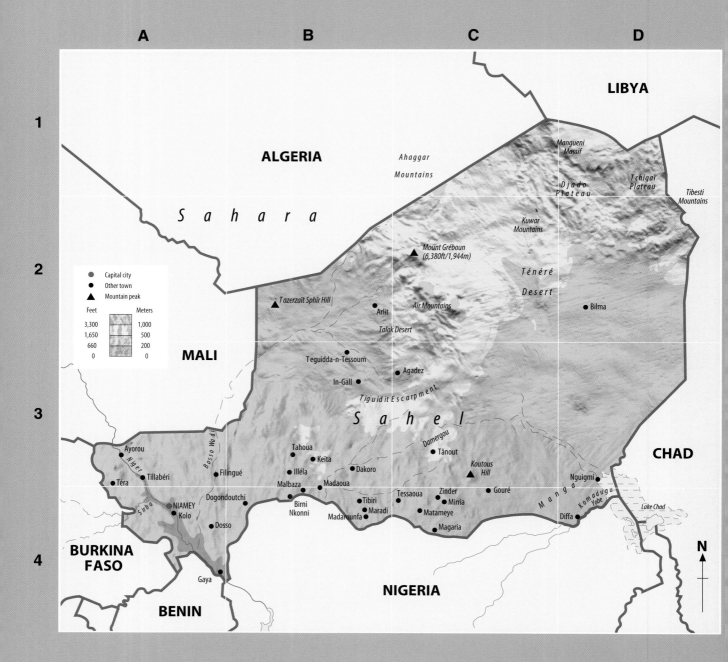

A **B** **C** **D**

1

2

3

4

LIBYA

ALGERIA

Ahaggar
Mountains

Mangueni
Massif

Djado
Plateau

T chigaï
Plateau

Tibesti
Mountains

S a h a r a

Kuwar
Mountains

▲ *Mount Gréboun*
(6,380ft/1,944m)

Ténéré

Desert

▲ *Tazerzaït Sphïr Hill*

• Arlit

Aïr Mountains

• Bilma

MALI

Talak Desert

Teguidda-n-Tessoum •

• Agadez

In-Gall •

Tiguidit Escarpment

S a h e l

Damergou

CHAD

● Capital city
● Other town
▲ Mountain peak

Feet		Meters
3,300		1,000
1,650		500
660		200
0		0

• Ayorou

Niger

Basso Wadi

Tahoua •
• Keita

• Tânout

Koutous
Hill ▲

• Tillabéri

• Filingué

Illéla •

• Dakoro

• Téra

Malbaza
Madaoua •

• Nguigmi

Manga

Komadougu
Yobe

NIAMEY
Kolo

Sirba

Dogondoutchi •

Birni
Nkonni

Tessaoua •

Zinder •
• Mirria

• Gouré

Lake Chad

Tibiri •
Maradi •

• Dosso

Madarounfa •

Matameye •

• Diffa

• Magaria

BURKINA
FASO

• Gaya

NIGERIA

N

BENIN

MAP OF NIGER

Agadez, C3
Ahaggar Mountains, C1
Aïr Mountains, C2
Algeria, A1—A2, B1—B2, C1—C2
Arlit, B2
Ayorou, A3

Benin, A4, B4
Bilma, D2
Birni Nkonni, B4
Bosso Wadi, A3
Burkina Faso, A3—A4

Chad, D1—D4
Chad, Lake, D3—D4

Dakoro, B3
Damergou River, C3
Diffa, D4

Djado Plateau, D1
Dogondoutchi, B4
Dosso, A4

Filingué, A3

Gaya, A4
Gouré, C4
Gréboun, Mount, C2

Illéla, B3
In-Gall, B3

Keïta, B3
Kolo, A4
Komadugu-Yobe River, D4
Koutous Hill, C3
Kuwar Mountains, C2, D2

Libya, C1, D1

Madaoua, B3, B4
Madaroumfa, B4
Magaria, C4
Malbaza, B4
Mali, A1—A3, B2—B3
Manga, C4, D3—D4
Mangueni Plateau, D1
Maradi, B4
Matameye, C4
Mirria, C4

Ngiuigmi, D3
Niamey, A4
Nigeria, B4, C4, D4
Niger River, A3—A4

Sahara, A2, B2
Sahel, B3, C3
Sirba River, A4

Tahoua, B3
Talak Desert, B2, C2
Tânout, C3
Tazerzaït Sphîr Hill, B2
Tchïgai Plateau, D1
Teguidda-n-Tessoum, B3
Ténéré Desert, C2, D2
Téra, A3
Tessaoua, C4
Tibesti Mountains, D1—D2
Tibiri, B4
Tiguidit Escarpment, B3, C3
Tillabéri, A3

Zinder, C4

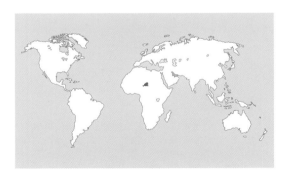

ECONOMIC NIGER

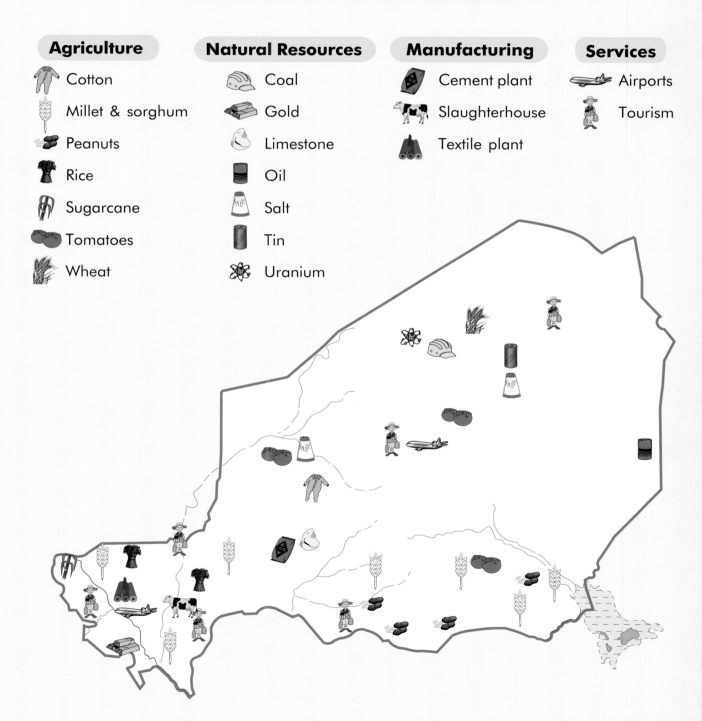

Agriculture
- Cotton
- Millet & sorghum
- Peanuts
- Rice
- Sugarcane
- Tomatoes
- Wheat

Natural Resources
- Coal
- Gold
- Limestone
- Oil
- Salt
- Tin
- Uranium

Manufacturing
- Cement plant
- Slaughterhouse
- Textile plant

Services
- Airports
- Tourism

ABOUT THE ECONOMY

All figures are 2017 estimates unless otherwise noted.

GROSS DOMESTIC PRODUCT (OFFICIAL EXCHANGE RATE)
$8.224 billion

GDP PER CAPITA
$1,200

GDP, BY SECTOR OF ORIGIN
Agriculture: 41.6 percent
Industry: 19.5 percent
Services: 38.7 percent

LABOR FORCE
6.5 million

LABOR FORCE, BY OCCUPATION
Agriculture: 79.2 percent
Industry: 3.3 percent
Services: 17.5 percent (2012)

UNEMPLOYMENT RATE
0.3 percent

POPULATION BELOW POVERTY LINE
45.4 percent (2014)

AGRICULTURAL PRODUCTS
Cowpeas, cotton, peanuts, millet, sorghum, cassava (tapioca), rice, cattle, sheep, goats, camels, donkeys, horses, poultry

INDUSTRIES
Uranium mining, petroleum, cement, brick, soap, textiles, food processing, chemicals, slaughterhouses

MAJOR EXPORTS
Uranium ore, livestock, cowpeas, onions

MAJOR IMPORTS
Foodstuffs, machinery, vehicles and parts, petroleum, grains

EXPORT PARTNERS
France 30.2 percent, Thailand 18.3 percent, Malaysia 9.9 percent, Nigeria 8.3 percent, Mali 5 percent, Switzerland 4.9 percent

IMPORT PARTNERS
France 28.8 percent, China 14.4 percent, Malaysia 5.7 percent, Nigeria 5.4 percent, Thailand 5.3 percent, US 5.1 percent, India 4.9 percent

CURRENCY
Communaute Financière Africaine franc (West African CFA franc) (XOF)
US $1 = 588.50 CFA franc (2019)

CULTURAL NIGER

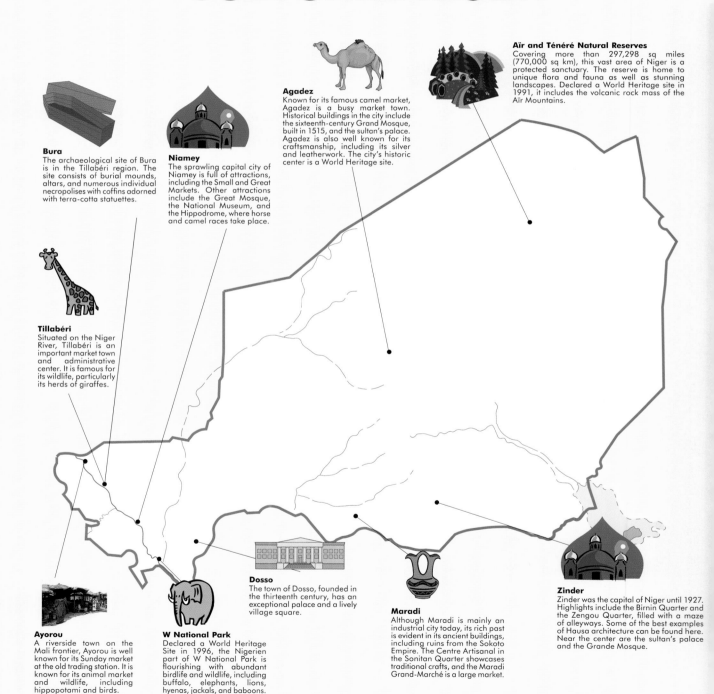

Aïr and Ténéré Natural Reserves
Covering more than 297,298 sq miles (770,000 sq km), this vast area of Niger is a protected sanctuary. The reserve is home to unique flora and fauna as well as stunning landscapes. Declared a World Heritage site in 1991, it includes the volcanic rock mass of the Aïr Mountains.

Agadez
Known for its famous camel market, Agadez is a busy market town. Historical buildings in the city include the sixteenth-century Grand Mosque, built in 1515, and the sultan's palace. Agadez is also well known for its craftsmanship, including its silver and leatherwork. The city's historic center is a World Heritage site.

Bura
The archaeological site of Bura is in the Tillabéri region. The site consists of burial mounds, altars, and numerous individual necropolises with coffins adorned with terra-cotta statuettes.

Niamey
The sprawling capital city of Niamey is full of attractions, including the Small and Great Markets. Other attractions include the Great Mosque, the National Museum, and the Hippodrome, where horse and camel races take place.

Tillabéri
Situated on the Niger River, Tillabéri is an important market town and administrative center. It is famous for its wildlife, particularly its herds of giraffes.

Ayorou
A riverside town on the Mali frontier, Ayorou is well known for its Sunday market at the old trading station. It is known for its animal market and wildlife, including hippopotami and birds.

W National Park
Declared a World Heritage Site in 1996, the Nigerien part of W National Park is flourishing with abundant birdlife and wildlife, including buffalo, elephants, lions, hyenas, jackals, and baboons.

Dosso
The town of Dosso, founded in the thirteenth century, has an exceptional palace and a lively village square.

Maradi
Although Maradi is mainly an industrial city today, its rich past is evident in its ancient buildings, including ruins from the Sokoto Empire. The Centre Artisanal in the Sonitan Quarter showcases traditional crafts, and the Maradi Grand-Marché is a large market.

Zinder
Zinder was the capital of Niger until 1927. Highlights include the Birnin Quarter and the Zengou Quarter, filled with a maze of alleyways. Some of the best examples of Hausa architecture can be found here. Near the center are the sultan's palace and the Grande Mosque.

ABOUT THE CULTURE

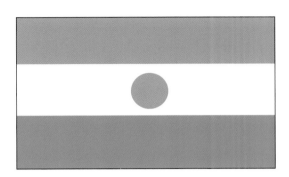

All figures are 2018 estimates unless otherwise noted.

OFFICIAL NAME
Republic of Niger

NATIONAL FLAG
Three equal horizontal bands of orange (top), white, and green with a small orange disk (representing the sun) centered in the white band; similar to the flag of India, which has a blue-spoked wheel centered in the white band

CAPITAL
Niamey

ADMINISTRATIVE DIVISIONS
Agadez, Diffa, Dosso, Maradi, Niamey, Tahoua, Tillabéri, Zinder

POPULATION
19,866,231 people

POPULATION GROWTH RATE
3.16 percent

LIFE EXPECTANCY AT BIRTH
Total population: 56.3 years
Male: 55 years
Female: 57.7 years

BIRTH RATE
43.6 births per 1,000 population

DEATH RATE
111.5 deaths per 1,000 population

ETHNIC GROUPS
Hausa, 53.1 percent; Zarma/Songhai, 21.2 percent; Tuareg, 11 percent; Fulani (Peuhl), 8.5 percent; Kanuri, 5.9 percent; Gurma, 0.8 percent; Arab, 0.4 percent; Tubu, 0.4 percent; other/unavailable, 0.9 percent (2006)

RELIGIONS
Muslim, 99.3 percent; Christian, 0.3 percent; animist, 0.2 percent; none, 0.1 percent (2012)

MAIN LANGUAGES
French (official), Hausa, Djerma

LITERACY RATE
Total population: 19.1 percent
Male: 27.3 percent
Female: 11 percent (2015)

MATERNAL MORTALITY RATE
553 deaths/100,000 live births (2015)

INFANT MORTALITY RATE
79.4 deaths/1,000 live births

TIMELINE

IN NIGER	IN THE WORLD
	1869 The Suez Canal is opened.
1890 France occupies Niger.	
	1914 World War I begins.
1922 Niger becomes a French colony.	
	1939 World War II begins.
	1945 The United States drops atomic bombs on Hiroshima and Nagasaki, Japan. World War II ends.
1958 Niger becomes an autonomous republic of the French Community.	
1960 Niger becomes independent. Hamani Diori is elected president.	
	1966 The Chinese Cultural Revolution.
1968–1973 Severe drought devastates Niger's economy, including its livestock and crop production.	
	1969 US astronauts land on the moon.
1974 Diori is overthrown in military coup led by Seyni Kountché.	
	1986 Nuclear power disaster at Chernobyl in Ukraine.
1987 Kountché dies of a brain tumor.	
1989 A new constitution brings Niger back to civilian rule, but under a one-party system.	
1990 President Ali Seybou legalizes opposition parties. Tuareg people in the north organize rebellion.	**1990** East Germany and West Germany are reunited as one country.
1991 A constitutional conference relieves Seybou of his powers.	**1991** Breakup of the Soviet Union.
1992 New constitution allowing multiparty elections is ratified.	
1993 Mahamane Ousmane is elected president.	
1995 Ceasefire between the government and the Tuareg's Revolutionary Armed Forces of the Sahara.	**1994** Nelson Mandela elected president in South Africa.

IN NIGER	IN THE WORLD
1996	
Ousmane ousted in a coup led by Ibrahim Maïnassara, who wins presidential election.	**1997** British return Hong Kong to China.
1999	
Following the assassination of Maïnassara, Mamadou Tandja is elected president.	**2001** Al-Qaeda terrorists attack the US on 9/11.
2003 Niger outlaws and criminalizes slavery.	**2003** War in Iraq begins.
2008 Police arrest former prime minister Hama Amadou on charges of embezzling state funds.	**2008** US elects first African American president, Barack Obama.
2009 Government and Tuareg rebels agree to end hostilities. Tandja suspends constitution and assumes emergency powers after Constitutional Court rules against his plans to seek a third term.	**2009** Outbreak of H1N1 flu around the world.
2010 Coup d'etat deposes Tandja.	
2011 Mahamadou Issoufou wins presidential elections. Tandja released from prison, charges dropped.	**2011** Earthquake and tsunami in northern Japan kills more than 15,000 people and causes nuclear reactor meltdowns at Fukushima power plant.
2013 Historical city of Agadez awarded World Heritage status by UNESCO.	
2016 Issoufou reelected. Boko Haram militants attack Bosso, killing 30.	**2015–2016** ISIS launches terror attacks in Belgium and France.
2017 Four US soldiers on a joint patrol with local troops are killed in an ambush near Tongo Tongo.	**2017** Donald Trump becomes US president. Hurricanes devastate Houston, Caribbean islands, and Puerto Rico.
2018 Italy's parliament approves the deployment of up to 470 troops in Niger to combat migration and the trafficking of people toward Europe.	**2018** Winter Olympics in South Korea.
2019 Boko Haram attack kills Nigerien soldiers in Diffa.	**2019** A terrorist attacks mosques in New Zealand.

GLOSSARY

bissap
Hibiscus tea or drink

egherdjira (ER-er-jee-rah)
A drink prepared with pounded millet, dates, milk, and goat cheese.

ezelé (ay-ZAY-lay)
A type of dance music played by Nigerien women.

griot
Local bard, poet, narrator, and musician.

hajj
The Muslim pilgrimage to Mecca.

harmattan
A desert wind.

hijab
A piece of cloth worn by a Muslim woman to cover her head and hair.

imam
A Muslim religious figure who preaches at a mosque.

inadan
Tuareg artisans.

marabouts
Quranic teachers.

sharro (SHAR-raw)
A physical competition that tests the endurance and bravery of Fulani teenagers.

tagelmust (tag-ERL-moost)
A piece of long, indigo cotton cloth worn by the Tuareg men to veil themselves.

teneghelt (te-NER-gelt)
A term used by the Tuaregs that refers to the silver cross of Agadez.

Tifinagh
An ancient script of the Berber language still used by the Tuareg.

tindé (TUHN-day)
Musical rhythm created by a tambourine-like instrument.

tô (TOH),
A popular West African dish made with white millet or sorghum balls.

wahaya
A form of sexual and domestic slavery that allows a man to take a "fifth wife." The women in such arrangements are also called wahaya.

Yenendi
A traditional ritual to summon rain when the rains fail to come at the end of the dry season.

FOR FURTHER INFORMATION

BOOKS

Geels, Jolijn. *Niger.* Bradt Travel Guides. Chalfont St. Peter, UK: Bradt Publications, 2006.

Jenkins, Mark. *To Timbuktu: A Journey Down the Niger.* London, UK: Robert Hale Ltd., 1998.

Kashi, Ed. *Curse of the Black Gold: 50 Years of Oil in the Niger Delta.* Brooklyn, NY: Powerhouse Books, 2008.

Rossi, Benedetta. *From Slavery to Aid: Politics, Labour, and Ecology in the Nigerien Sahel, 1800— 2000.* Cambridge, UK: Cambridge University Press, 2015.

Stoller, Paul. *Yaya's Story: The Quest for Well-Being in the World.* Chicago: University of Chicago Press, 2014.

FILMS

Niger. Dan Balluff Film and Video Production, 2005.

Niger. CustomFlix, 2007.

One Day in Africa. Earthchild Productions, 2009

MUSIC

Etran Finatawa. "Tekana" (Niger) from the album *Think Global: Celebrate Africa!* Think Global/World Music Network, 2009.

Group Bombino. *Guitars from Agadez.* Music of Niger, vol. 2. Sublime Frequencies/Forced Exp., 2009.

Group Inerane. *Guitars from Agadez.* Music of Niger, vol. 1. Sublime Frequencies/Forced Exp., 2008.

Group Inerane. *Guitars from Agadez.* Music of Niger, vol. 3. Sublime Frequencies/Forced Exp., 2011.

Various Artists. *Folk Music of the Sahel 1: Niger.* Sublime Frequencies/Forced Exp., 2014.

ONLINE

Afrobarometer. http://afrobarometer.org/countries/niger-01.

Al Jazeera. "Niger News." https://www.aljazeera.com/topics/country/niger.html.

BBC News. "Niger Country Profile." https://www.bbc.com/news/world-africa-13943662.

CIA. *The World Factbook.* "Niger." https://www.cia.gov/library/publications/the-world-factbook/geos/ng.html.

Encyclopaedia Britannica. "Niger." https://www.britannica.com/place/Niger.

Guardian. Niger archives. https://www.theguardian.com/world/niger.

New York Times. Niger archives. https://www.nytimes.com/topic/destination/niger.

BIBLIOGRAPHY

Abdelkader, Galy Kadir, ed. "Slavery in Niger." Anti-Slavery International and Association Timidira. https://www.antislavery.org/wp-content/uploads/2017/01/full_english_slavery_in_niger.pdf.

AllAfrica. Africa: "Salifou Fatimata Bazeye, Jurist Who Backed Democracy in Niger, Named 'African of the Year.'" December 4, 2011. https://allafrica.com/stories/201112040044.html.

BBC News. "Niger Country Profile." https://www.bbc.com/news/world-africa-13943662.

Bradshaw Foundation. "The Tuareg of the Sahara." http://www.bradshawfoundation.com/tuareg/index.php.

Bybee, Ashley Neese. "Niger: The Golden Desert." *Africa Watch*, November 1, 2018. https://www.ida.org/~/media/Corporate/Files/Publications/AfricaWatch/Africawatch-November-1-2018-vol21.pdf.

CIA. *The World Factbook*. "Niger." https://www.cia.gov/library/publications/the-world-factbook/geos/ng.html.

Destrijcker, Lucas, and Mahadi Diouara. "A Forgotten Community: The Little Town in Niger Keeping the Lights on in France." *African Arguments*, July 18, 2017. https://africanarguments.org/2017/07/18/a-forgotten-community-the-little-town-in-niger-keeping-the-lights-on-in-france-uranium-arlit-areva.

Eilerts, Gary. "Niger 2005: Not a Famine, But Something Much Worse." Humanitarian Practices Network, April 2006. https://odihpn.org/magazine/niger-2005-not-a-famine-but-something-much-worse.

Encyclopaedia Britannica. "Niger." https://www.britannica.com/place/Niger.

Ethnologue. "Niger." https://www.ethnologue.com/country/ne.

Felbab-Brown, Vanda. "In the Eye of the Storm: Niger and its Unstable Neighbors." Brookings, June 13, 2017. https://www.brookings.edu/blog/order-from-chaos/2017/06/13/in-the-eye-of-the-storm-niger-and-its-unstable-neighbors.

Global Slavery Index 2018. https://www.globalslaveryindex.org/2018/findings/global-findings.

Schmitt, Eric. "A Shadowy War's Newest Front: A Drone Base Rising From Saharan Dust." *New York Times*, April 18, 2018. https://www.nytimes.com/2018/04/22/us/politics/drone-base-niger.html.

Guardian. "Areva's Uranium Mining Deal with Niger Receives Cautious Welcome." May 28, 2014. https://www.theguardian.com/global-development/2014/may/28/areva-niger-uranium-mining-deal.

Quist-Arcton, Ofeibea. "In Grip of Drought, Floods, Niger Faces Hunger Crisis." NPR, August 20, 2010. https://www.npr.org/templates/story/story.php?storyId=129316900.

Whiting, Alex. "Warming May Turn Africa's Arid Sahel Green: Researchers." *Climate Central*, July 8, 2017. https://www.climatecentral.org/news/climate-change-africas-arid-sahel-green-21602.

INDEX

INDEX